It's Good to B-

Christina Chase

IT'S GOOD TO BE HERE

*A Disabled Woman's Reflections
on God in the Flesh and the
Sacred Wonder of Being Human*

SOPHIA INSTITUTE PRESS
Manchester, New Hampshire

Sophia Institute Press

Box 5284, Manchester, NH 03108

1-800-888-9344

www.SophiaInstitute.com

Sophia Institute Press® is a registered trademark of Sophia Institute.

Library of Congress Cataloging-in-Publication Data

Names: Chase, Christina, author.

Title: It's good to be here : a disabled woman's reflections on God in the flesh and the sacred wonder of being human / Christina Chase.

Description: Manchester, New Hampshire : Sophia Institute Press, 2019. | Summary: "A disabled woman's reflections on God in the flesh and the sacred wonder of being human"— Provided by publisher.

Identifiers: LCCN 2019046145 | ISBN 9781644131077 | ISBN 9781644131084 (ebook)

Subjects: LCSH: People with disabilities—Religious life. | God (Christianity)—Worship and love. | Disabilities—Religious aspects—Christianity.

Classification: LCC BV4910 .C43 2019 | DDC 248.8/64—dc23

LC record available at https://lccn.loc.gov/2019046145

First printing

Dedicated to the Sacred Heart of Jesus,
in thanksgiving for
my amazing, self-giving parents,
Dan and Francine,
who have helped me to know that I am loved,
and for Carole, Carl, Matthew, and Nathan,
who are also loving wonders in my life

The glory of God is a human being fully alive, and the life of a human being is the beholding of God.

—St. Irenaeus, *Against Heresies*, bk. 4, 20:7

Contents

Crippled: A Preface

This little book contains reflections from a human person who loves the gift of life, with all of its fearful wonder, and who is diseased and disabled. These personal reflections, both the long and the short of them, some adapted from blog posts and some written specifically for this book, have as their focus the loving wonder of life—the meaning of being human and the amazing privilege, goodness, and sacred joy of being here in God's Creation. Christ, who is both fully divine and fully human, shows us not only who God is, but also who we are in the divine living of His little life on Earth. After all, this is the place where God, the Creator of the universe, chose to live *in the flesh*.

Like a little manger, crudely fashioned by human hands, the pages of this book hold God Incarnate, God in the flesh, in the fragile state of His humanity, full of newness, wonder, and love of life. The Creator of all chose to become a helpless and dependent creature, experiencing our suffering, our sorrows, and our delights because He infinitely loves each and every one of us and wants to pull us ever more intimately into the power and bliss of His divine love.

I know that I cannot do Christ justice—all that I can do is simply love Him. In loving Him, however, I realize my true identity and reason for being human, and I'm filled with the wonder and goodness of being alive. Beginning with the wonder of created life and our human need for divine love, this book chronologically explores Christ's life on Earth, from conception, through infancy, adolescence, and adulthood, ending with Christ's present life among us in the world. Each section is introduced with a personal reflection on some aspect of my own little life on Earth, because God became incarnate in order to unite Himself wholly with us in our little lives.

My life is very little. In the subtitle of this book, I have identified myself as a disabled woman, but I often refer to myself as a cripple. My genetic, lifespan-shortening disease (SMA type II) makes me physically dependent on others and incredibly weak—certainly a cripple. (Forget political correctness.) Although, if we met in person, my crumpled, crippled body in a wheelchair would probably be the first thing that you would notice about me, I don't share this fact as an introduction to who I am—for I am so much more than what my body can't do. We are not meant to *define* ourselves by our limitations, but always, in wise humility and desire for truth, we are meant to acknowledge them—with love. Everybody is unique, but I have always known and felt my rarity because of my progressive muscle-wasting disease. Being so obviously different from other people gives me an unusual perspective on what it truly means to be fully human.

All humans are limited by virtue of being creatures: we cannot exist without definitions, boundaries. We are all dependent—on God, our Source, and on God's Creation—and every human person is helpless in the face of forces beyond our control. In our pride, we like to think that we can control anything and everything that we put our minds to and that we should exist independently, self-sufficient and autonomous, made for our own finite ends. But we are made for endless glory—we are made for divine love. Through our self-centeredness, we often miss this mark. We sin. Our pride hinders us from living the fullness of reality.

And so, we are all cripples.

Nobody can walk through this life unaided.

And none of us, through our own power, can stand in the presence of God.

In the full embrace of truth, I know that all of us who live and breathe as part of this fearsomely wonderful Creation are crippled in some way. We desire. We need. We lack. With our struggles and sufferings, our stories might be tragic—but for the fact that we are infinitely *loved*. This love is the source of our human dignity. Our true joy and fulfillment abide in the receiving and giving of divine love, now and forever.

For God so loves the world that He became one of us, incarnate. *O Wonder of wonders!* Our fears He lived, and He showed us that we need not be afraid. Even the less-than-wonderful aspects of being human have been made sacred and terribly beautiful because God Himself has *lived* them *in the flesh*. Almighty God became human—to raise us to the divine, both now, in the living of life here on this blessed earth, and forever, in the perfect glory of God's love.

It's Good to Be Here

Here I Am, Lord

On the Wonder of Being:
The Mystery of the Incarnation,
the Nativity of Christ, and the Hidden Years,
Introduced by My X-Ray Image

Fearfully and Wonderfully

One look at my weak, twisted body, and it's pretty obvious that I'm a mess.

Chatting and laughing with my family doctor at a regular appointment one day, I took the time to look closely at my X-ray images, and even I was a bit shocked by what I saw. My ribs and right hip have extensive deformities; the spine in my thorax is nearly horizontal and rotated so that the spinal cord is on the side; and the vertebrae are misshapen, lacking discs to cushion, and riddled with arthritis. Deeply studying the images of my bones as a woman near forty, having lived my original life expectancy three times over, I said aloud, "How does that not hurt more?"

And I wondered to myself: *How am I alive?*

Conceived with a particular genetic flaw, a defect unwittingly passed on to me by both of my parents, I have a crippling disease called Spinal Muscular Atrophy, which causes a severe shriveling up of muscles as my motor nerve cells progressively deteriorate. Born into the world a seemingly healthy baby, my body slowly weakened every year, never able to walk, losing gross and fine motor skills, and collapsing upon itself with severe scoliosis. My weak neck is bent over with my sharply S-shaped spine so that, as I sit crumpled up in my wheelchair, my head rests heavily upon my left shoulder and hunched back.

Never having walked, I can't say that I miss the ability, but that doesn't mean that I don't *want* it. I most certainly want it. Still, it's the progressive collapsing and weakening of my body that is the worst part of the disease. The yearly losses of strength and abilities — lifting up my arms, feeding myself, brushing my own teeth, breathing without labor — these are the hardest things to bear. "Hard to bear" is an understatement. The difficulties, disappointments, and deteriorations can be overwhelming ... and sad. Terrifyingly sad. The circumstances of my life altered my childhood, undermined my teenage years, and rendered me into an adult who is completely dependent upon others for everyday survival. My body has been wracked with the pain of angry weeping, my bones crying out with shuddering grief, and my mind seized with the heartache of my life. And yet ...

I am not bitter.

I pine for independence, for a family of my own, and I mourn the physical losses, the sickness, the shortened life span. And yet ...

I do not despair.

I get madly frustrated by my illness and disability, and I sorrow deeply for the "nevers" of my life. And yet ...

I am very glad to be here.

Why am I glad? I ask myself. Even I wonder at how I can be the generally content, grateful, and joyful person that I am. Over and over, I have asked myself why I, cripple that I am, continue to have a deep love for life.

Why?

Because I am fearfully and wonderfully made.[1]

---

[1] See Psalm 139:14.

To be alive … to be alive is the gift divine, profound, and unfathomably, terribly beautiful. I need not exist at all, but I do! To be alive … to be alive is the rarest of gifts, for there is only one me, and *I* am me. No one else. There is not, and never will be, another me in all of the vast and mighty stretches of the cosmos, the billions of galaxies, the multitude of universes that may have existed or may come into existence. Just *one*. Just *me*. Particularly, *exquisitely* unique.

Here am I.

Some people wish that they had never been born, especially those who suffer physically, mentally, or emotionally. I know people who have had their lives severely limited by disabilities who would rather have never existed. But I don't know what that's like. I have never had such a desire or wish. Could it be because I haven't experienced enough pain in my life? There are, after all, billions of ways to suffer in this world, as many kinds of pain as there are people. And yet …

No one else's sufferings are particularly mine. Similarly, no one else's delights are particularly mine. My sufferings and my joys are my own in that *I* live them. I live the ups and downs of my life, the struggles and the wonders, singularly unique to *me*. And *I* am alive. I am *alive*.

I am alive!

Do you hear that? Do you feel that?

Do you *know* that?

I am alive. Here I am, fearfully and wonderfully made by the Creator and Master of All. Let everyone be struck with fear. The whole world trembles and the heavens exalt[2]—because *I* am. I am *alive*.

[2] See St. Francis of Assisi, *Letter to All the Friars*.

Messy.
Real.
Unique.
Here.
Fearfully and wonderfully human.

God So Loved the World

Why do we say that life is a gift and God is love?

There is so much suffering in the mess of our aching world
— through war, plagues, and corruption, in sickness, abuse, and
loneliness — that we may well feel that God is cold and distant.
We may doubt the goodness of being here. Suffering my own
particular pain and heartbreak, I have at times turned in upon
myself, mourning the unwanted situation of my life of progressive disease and severe disability. There is an isolating, dark, and
brutal kind of hardness in such heartache that seems to suck the
air out of everything, and we cannot see or hear even a hint of
joy in life. *Why?* I have asked. Like all of suffering humankind,
I want to know why we exist at all.

In the midst of anger, grief, and melancholy, we suffer the
confines of our agonizing world, closing in on ourselves as we
look for answers and question the point of Creation. Relying on
ourselves alone, our seeking is terminally limited, ending in our
finite selves, and we are sadly deafened, blinded, and numbed
to the fullness of life by our very struggling. We are not made
for such isolation, for such futility. We are here for the *fullness*
of life, of truth — we exist for divine love.

It's Good to Be Here

The Gift of the Cosmos

Before I came to the understanding that God is love, I would sit beneath the night sky, crumpled up in my wheelchair, filled with wonder at the vastness of the cosmos, and feel my heart effervesce into the stars. There was a glimpse of communion with the mystery of God's self-giving love in this, but I did not recognize it. I merely felt enthralled by the awareness of both my own littleness and the bigness of the world at the same time, knowing that I am tiny and dependent upon a massive planet, which is miniscule in a gargantuan galaxy, which is but a speck in a far-flung universe. Being even more pitifully limited without recognition of divine love, the terrible beauty of the cosmos seemed enough for me, and I ventured no further.

But I am made for more.

After recognition, contemplation of the stars became exquisitely more breathtaking and euphoric, and for a profoundly deeper reason: existence is not merely vast, but *infinite*.

As clever and resourceful as we humans are, we did not create ourselves, and we are utterly dependent upon what God has made. In the midst of a raging storm, upon the sunny slopes of a blossoming valley, or beneath the deep and starry sky, we can observe the observable with our physical senses, and with our tools and calculations we can discern something of the *how* of the created world. This is good, but our sense of wonder inspires us to seek further. Unable to penetrate beyond the created forces and things of the universe, however, we cannot scientifically know the *why* of its existence — or of our own.

Only the key of sacred wonder can open the mystery of *why*. It is discovered by first finding not ourselves, but God. Before humans came to be, before the Earth came to be, before the universe came to be, there was the ultimate reality "that everyone calls God."[3] As an ancient Hebrew proverb states, "The fear of the LORD is the beginning of wisdom."[4] This doesn't mean that we will only have true understanding if we shake and cower in fright whenever we think of God's power over us. *Not exactly.* But we do need to recognize and respect that power. Think about it: we are at the mercy of an invisible, immortal, all-knowing, and all-powerful deity who brought a trillion-galaxied universe and every particle of every atom into existence out of nothing, by sheer will, and who has the power to terminate the lives of all the living in an instant.

Does that sound a little scary?

Excellent.

True fear of the Lord is realizing that God *is* God, and we most certainly *are not.*

To see the fullness of our lives, therefore, to know why we exist and to understand the real goodness of being here even in the midst of pain, we need to begin with the beginning—with *who* God is.

With no beginning and no end, God is pure spirit, Being itself, perfectly self-sufficient in all goodness and rightness—nothing other than God needs to exist. The fact of the universe's existence alone is cause for endless awe. God didn't have to create anything, *but He did.*

Why?

God so *loved* the world that He created it.

By creating, God freely chose to give something other than Himself the gift of existence, the gift of Being—the gift of

---

[3] *Catechism of the Catholic Church*, no. 34.
[4] Proverbs 9:10 (NIV).

Himself. Creation, therefore, is truly understood as an act of *self-giving* for the sake of the other: an act of *love*. God's love is so profoundly generous as to generate energy, matter, and all life. Through His divine say-so, God establishes the universe, shapes our lovely, lively little planet, and forms each and every living creature—including you and me.

The Bible's book of Genesis poetically illustrates God's power to create the cosmos as an effortless and joyful breathing of His Word:

> In the beginning, when God created the
>   heavens and the earth....
> God said: Let there be light, and there was light.
> God saw that the light was good....
> Then God said: Let there be ...
>   sky ...
>   earth ...
>   sea ...
>   every kind of plant ...
>   tree ...
>   stars ...
>   an abundance of living creatures....
> God created mankind in his image;
> in the image of God he created them;
> male and female he created them ...
> blessed them ...
> And so it happened.
> God looked at everything he had made, and
>   found it very good.[5]

---

[5] Genesis 1:1, 3–4, 6, 8, 10, 11, 16, 20, 27–28, 30–31.

The Gift of Humankind

Although we may sometimes doubt it, especially in times of great sorrow and distress, God didn't create life on Earth to be a drudgery or misery. God didn't make us human beings merely to suffer and die. God made us for good. From all of the lifeforms that He brought into being on Earth — those teeming beneath the sea, creeping in the fields and forests, and flying through the air — God chose to make human beings significantly different.

Why?

God so loved the world that He wanted to *share* it.

So that we could be *persons*, freely accepting and sharing God's love, God created us in His own image, forming us not only of matter — of flesh — but also of spirit — of *Himself* — with immortal souls and the godlike gifts of intellect and free will. Participation in divine love is beyond animal instinct and cannot be forced, because, freely given, God's love must be freely recognized and received. God's will for us, our reason for being, is to realize that we are particularly and eternally loved by our Creator, to freely receive and return that love, to personally appreciate and participate in the beloved goodness of Creation, and to experience now and forever the divine fulfillment of giving ourselves to others in love. In genuinely living as God's images, we are *fully* human, partaking of God's eternal life of love, experiencing the profound joy — the *paradise* — of life.

That is *why* we are here. But we know painfully well that it's not *how* we live here, in the mess that our world has become. Why is that?

The reason is also love.

The gift of life, the gift of divine love, is so great a gift that it comes at a great risk. With our God-given intellect, we humans have the ability to seek, recognize, and deeply know God's loving presence and purposes, but also to become completely absorbed by our physical senses and finite concerns, and so fail to see the full goodness of life in all of its rich complexity. With our God-given free will, we have the ability to freely accept God's love for us and joyfully participate in the divine life by giving ourselves in love, but also to reject God's love and turn away from our very reason for being, and so reduce the world, one another — and ourselves — to mere objects of finite usefulness.

That's what happened in the nascent development of human consciousness. Created to be God-centered, centered in the fullness of truth and divine love, we have instead become self-centered, and life has been put out of order.

The inspired book of Genesis[6] pictures our first parents fully enjoying the amazing abundance of Creation and living in innocent, loving familiarity with God and each other, until they failed to *trust* in God's love. Seeing that God is all-knowing and humans are not, our original ancestors failed to use their God-given intellect to appreciate the necessity of this difference — God is God, and what God creates cannot be God — and failed to employ their God-given free will to embrace their sacred littleness in the fullness of the gift of life. Instead, they were tempted to think that God was holding back His gifts from them, and they chose to go against God's will in an attempt to gain divine power for themselves.

The reason that we are hurting so badly here in the mess of our world is that we have become separated from the infinite and eternal source of true life and true love. Torn away from God's loving will, from the full goodness of His plan, a rift has developed

---

[6] See Genesis 2:4–25, 3.

between human life and divine life, and the gifts that we have from God depreciated because of the division. It's like we've inherited a disorder that causes crippling damage to our souls, darkening our intellect and weakening our will. The natural limitations that we necessarily experience as creatures have become overwhelming sufferings that they were not intended to be, and the world in which we live has become horribly broken by the self-centered, sinful actions of humans who have lost intimacy with God, with the self-giving power of real love.

The Gift of Being Human

We may be tempted to think that God should use His might to force us to acknowledge Him and love Him always, so that we would never lose sight of true goodness, never do harm, and always love and care for each other in our littleness. However, God cannot force us to do anything without destroying our gifts of free will and intellect—our very ability to participate in His love and know the real joy of life. To live here in God's terribly beautiful Creation as divine images is a blessed privilege that necessarily includes limitations—limitations that God will not break because our sacred littleness is too unfathomably precious. Each and every human being is worthy of experiencing God's eternal love, now and forever, because each and every human being *is eternally loved.* So as long as there is life in us, there is hope for us. Therefore, God will neither destroy us nor abandon us to the effects of sin.

Everybody wants a miracle. Everybody wants to be spared pain by God, making everything heartbreaking go away. God knows that I have begged for this in my misery. However, constant divine intervention would cease to be miraculous, and, most essentially, this earth would cease to be the place where we learn how to give of ourselves in love—*to be like God*—the place where we share in the divine life.

God knew the risk of creating us for eternal love, but He freely chose to do so because He also knew that we could be saved from falling endlessly away from divine love—from Him—through one last, ultimate gift of Himself. To prepare humankind to receive such a gift, God first gave the ancients the gift of His Word through prophets, communicating to them in a language that they could understand in the fallen and damaged state of their souls, cultivating a relationship with a family that grew into a tribe and then a nation. He instilled a fear of the Lord in the Hebrew people and, when they listened, gave them His Word of eternal love, promising that He would mercifully heal the rift between humanity and divinity, restoring humankind to true life in the divine image, to paradise without end.

Then, God Almighty, Creator and Master of the cosmos and beyond, made His Word a flesh-and-blood reality by doing something downright preposterous and seemingly ridiculous.

God came *here*. God chose to become *one of us*.

> In the beginning was the Word
> and the Word was with God
> and the Word was God.
> He was in the beginning with God.
> All things came to be through him,
> and without him nothing came to be.
> And the Word became flesh
> and made his dwelling among us.[7]

---

[7] John 1:1–3, 14.

The divine Word, who spoke light and life into existence, became a human being—divine Son of divine Father. Fearsome and eternal God personally entered our lives, born into our hurting world to live here with us. Not as a fierce warrior or human ruler of indisputable right did God choose to live here, but truly *as one of us*, a rather ordinary man with family and friends, with enemies and suffering.

Why?

God so *loved* the world that He chose to live in it.

Doubts of God's love vanish in the light of Jesus Christ—*God in the flesh*. Omnipotent and omniscient God, Creator of billions upon billions of galaxies, infinite God whom we mistrust and even disdain in our darkened perception and sufferings, came down from limitlessness in order to divinely live the sacred littleness of one human life. For the goodness of being here, God chose to intimately, *humanly* experience the beauty and happiness of the world that divine love created, as well as the limitations, burdens, human cruelty, and painful sorrows of our fallen-away lives—*to suffer with us*—experiencing His own excruciating agony.

What else is this but love? God loves us little human beings enough to humbly give of Himself, not only by giving us the gift of Creation and the gift of *being* in His divine image of love, but also by giving Himself *personally*, totally, and perpetually, living in intimate union with us, His beloved creatures, now and forever. Christ, fully human and fully divine, heals the division between divinity and humanity by suffering the effects of our sins and laying Himself down in the rift.

How far does God go to prove His love for us, revealing the goodness of the gift of life? God comes down even into the very depths of our pain and sorrows, so far that He who is immortal tasted death in order to bring us back to true life. *O most holy Wonder of wonders.*

The Gift

Our world remains the mess that it is, and our hearts still break. In our pain, we naturally question and even doubt, *but the gift remains.* Suffering itself is a mystery, which cannot be fully explored or understood by our limited and finite means as we struggle in the dark. Suffering—like all of life, including experiences of great joy—has its ultimate meaning revealed in Christ: God in the flesh, love incarnate. The one astonishing fact of life is that suffering, like disease, war, murder, and abuse, cannot destroy the gift that God Almighty gives, because real love never fails. Love is as immortal as God Himself. Through Christ Crucified and Resurrected, we know that those whom we mourn are not lost, and those who hurt us cannot destroy us, for God so loves the world that the fearsomely wonderful gift of divinely loved human life will never end.

No matter how long we study or contemplate the sands and the stars, our limited senses and intellect cannot unravel this mystery. The fullness of the gift of life is revealed, lived, and given through Christ, who is both God and human. Only God can reveal the mystery and give this gift to us because God *is* the gift. In knowing and loving Christ here and now, we come to know and love God—and ourselves.

Beloved, let us love one another, because love is of God; everyone who loves is begotten by God and knows God. Whoever is without love does not know God, for God is love. In this way the love of God was revealed to us:

God sent his only Son into the world so that we might have life through him.[8]

Through sacred wonder and the gift of faith, I know that my human heart and yours beat with the pulsating of starlight, the crashing of waves on rocky shores, and the burgeoning of blossoms in the springtime, as well as with the embryonic fluttering, the passionate throbbing, and the ultimate piercing of Christ's own Sacred Heart giving ever anew the gift of life to God's beloved world.

> All things came to be through him,
> and without him nothing came to be.
> What came to be through him was life,
> and this life was the light of the human race;
> the light shines in the darkness,
> and the darkness has not overcome it.[9]

---

[8] 1 John 4:7–9, emphasis added.
[9] John 1:3–5.

Among the Smells and Ills

Being human can be very messy. We all suffer, or will suffer, from one weakness or another, from aches, pains, deteriorations, and deficiencies of countless kinds. The human body is fragile and complex, but also amazing. In the prime of life, humans are physically capable of strength and finesse, speed and stealth, force and tenderness. With graceful curves and agile motion, expressive eyes, glistening skin, sensitive lips and fingertips, the human body is beautiful in many ways. But it isn't always pretty.

Think about it. The basic actions that we *all* need to survive—chewing, toileting, washing away sweat, dirt, and dead skin from our bodies—are a bit, well ... gross. We all poop. We all stink. There's nothing pretty about any of this daily reality of being human, nothing dreamy, romantic, or ennobling.

And yet ...

The pure, perfect, divine Creator of the universe chose to become a lowly human being.

God loves us this much: *to be like us*, to take human flesh upon His Divine Person, to live within the confines of an earthly form, dependent upon the functions of survival—eating, drinking, excreting, washing, sleeping, waking. *This is my Lord and my God.*

How many people who call themselves Christians are truly mindful of this, of the profound and awesome *shock* of the Incarnation? This is no small thing that we believe. This is no mere trifling of fancy that makes for an entertaining story to tell. We believe that God, infinite and eternal, Creator of all, became incarnate, humbling Himself to become *one of us*. The Word of God was made *flesh*, becoming a human being who knew poverty, hunger, thirst, sweat, dirt, fatigue, and pain; who knew familial love, friendship, laughter, and pleasure; who knew loss, sorrow, rejection, ridicule, betrayal, hatred, dread, and agony; a human being who was falsely accused, tortured, and killed, asphyxiated to death. And He did it all, He suffered it all, *for love*—for love of *you*.

No human mind can truly comprehend this. No human can fully grasp and appreciate the meaning and full impact of this—no way, no how. We can only be in awe and marvel in exuberant wonder at *God with us*. To love human beings this much—enough for God to empty Himself[10] and to be born human, in a human body with all of the smells and ills—is simply unfathomable.

Reflecting upon the incarnate love of God reveals the sacred beauty and dignity of our own humanness. Choosing to take on flesh and come bodily among us, God wanted to live every aspect of being human, right from the very beginning, and so, like us, He had a very real mother, though she was a mother like no other. The conception of divine love in the flesh began through her pure and free choice to receive God's Word, and from her flesh and her blood He took form and shape in her virginal womb. In the divine pregnancy, we see that God is completely with us, even in the most miniscule human state, experiencing our most fragile vulnerability and dependency.

[10] See Philippians 2:7.

In the beginning of His human life, limitless, infinite God was infinitesimally small, as we all begin. His human heart first beat while He was the size of a sesame seed. In the hidden world of the womb, the Creator developed His own eyes with which to look and see from within Creation, beginning with the dim light that penetrated through His mother's body. He developed His own little ears with which to hear, first the sounds of His mother's heartbeat and then muffled voices and music, learning and loving as He listened. Taste buds grew for the enjoying of food, giving God His first taste of sweets and bitters through amniotic fluid, flavored with the meals of figs, olives, lentils, and fish that His mother ate. The legs and feet with which He would walk along Galilean shores and march up to Calvary first kicked and danced in the watery world of His forming, while His human hands with all of their little fingers were taking shape, hands that would give God the ability to touch. The first thing that God physically touched was His own human face.

God didn't even choose to be born in a palace or luxurious hospital, like we may have done if we had the choice. God Incarnate chose as His birthplace a stable where animals lived. Do you know the smell of a stable? Can you imagine? Animals that urinate and defecate where they stand, that belch and snort and try to scratch their crusty hides, huddled in a closed off space made warm only by the heat of their bodies. There, in piles of hay, God Incarnate was birthed from His mother in the very real and particular mess and fragility of childbirth. God didn't choose luxury as His first bed. God chose, as His sleeping place, a crude feeding trough, edges chewed and worn by animal teeth, some of their saliva and mucus smearing the sides. God chose to live in the mess.

There among His own warm-bodied creatures of pasture and pen, their dark eyes reflecting the fire of lamplight like deep forest pools, there with the winged insects beyond the opening of the stable chirping a serenade while the silver stars twinkled above, there in a single small spot of His own created Earth, the Word of God made flesh drew His first breath of air. The Creator was born a creature, subject to the womb, to birth, to helpless infancy, to the care of His human mother who bore Him. His mom, with the immaculate love of her heart and the amazing goodness of her female body, kissed her little baby, *her divine Lord*, and nourished Him with the richness of mother's milk.

God — who laid the cornerstone of the universe, caused the stars to sing, formed the raiment of clouds, set the sea in its boundaries, and made to leap all of the wild things of Earth — was swaddled and immobilized by a few strips of cloth. *O Wonder of wonders*. God who placed the planets in their revolutions was placed, a helpless newborn, in a manger of hay to sleep. And sleep He needed, for His small eyelids grew tired as His little muscles whimpered for rest.

It's a big world for a tiny human being, especially *this* tiny baby, who had much to experience, much to enjoy and to suffer, and so very much to *love*.

Childlike Wonder

In the autumn, I like to drive my power wheelchair up the driveway of my home for the sole purpose of coming back down through the fallen leaves, which the wind furrows at the edges of the asphalt. That crisp, crackling sound of autumn underfoot (or under wheel), with the few remnants of golden leaves clinging to the bare limbs overhead, always elicits within me a feeling of merriment and the rhythm of mirth. Often, however, I wonder what others think of me, looking at me, an adult, going out of my way like that in order to maneuver my wheelchair over dry leaves. Some patronizing passersby may look at me as intellectually disabled as well as physically, or some may merely think that I am pitifully immature.

But I do it anyway.

To zigzag a sidewalk just to crunch the fallen maple leaves; to drive through the colorful drifts on rural roads; to rake up piles of the brittle bygones and let someone (maybe yourself) jump in them is pure delight. Perhaps the ones who are immature are those who consider this delight childish, while it is considered simply and blessedly *childlike* by those who are fully alive in the sacred wonder of being human.

"I tell you the truth, unless you change and become like little children, you will never enter the kingdom of heaven."[11] Scholars tell us that these words of Jesus from the Gospel of St. Matthew have to do with childlike *trust* and not the wonder and joy of children. Reflecting on this, however, we can see how wonder and joy *come from that trust.* Children are free from worry when they trustingly put their lives in the hands of their loving parents, and this freedom, gained through faith, allows them to be more open to wonder and joy.

This is what God, our Eternal Father, intends for us throughout our lives.

Our brains start off little and fluid, synapses sparking and connections made every time we experience something new. The things we perceive as children make impressions on our minds, forming not only our memories, but also our ways of reacting to the vast variety of stimuli and situations, as well as our ways of thinking about ourselves and others. Every new experience creates a response that forms our minds and hearts.

We are shaped by wonder.

Wonder is innately human; every child experiences it, even those who suffer from limited perception or diminished cognition. Wonder is an essential part of being human, as our souls are made for seeking and experiencing the good, the true, and the beautiful—for seeking and experiencing the Divine. Christ, fully divine though He was, was also fully human. Although as God and the Word of God, He created the trees, the rivers, and the birds, He did not experience them with the joyful awe and wonder of a human being until He became incarnate—until He became *fully human.*

[11] See Matthew 18:3.

Yes, Jesus Christ, Lord and Savior of the world, was once a real child, with the full human capacity to wonder.

As His loving mother cradled Him in her arms, singing softly to Him, He cooed with pleasure, gazing up into her tender eyes while His own learned to focus. The dipping flight of brightly colored birds must have lit the imagination of the little boy, joyfully kicking His baby legs upon Mary's knee. How many birds did He startle into flight when He first began to run, His own pulse rising with the fluttering of their wings? The sultry scent of summer's twilight, heavy with blossoms and ripening fruit, stirred within the growing youth the sweet ache of beauty and a deep sense of longing and mourning. How many thick leaves did He pull from bushes to crush within His hand, the sharp pungency clearing His mind to marvel at the tender, green flesh upon His own?

Learning for hours beside His loving foster father, Joseph, surrounded by the many fragrances of split trees, the rhythmic hewing and planing of timber and board made impressions in Jesus's memory, as He swept up curls of wood from the floor. When grown, He worked for a living, and His muscles got strong and sore as He built things with rough and calloused hands, smoothing fine grains and hoisting beams upon His shoulders.

Jesus experienced many wonders in His life here. He submerged His body in clear running waters, felt both the desert sun and the sea wind on His face, gratefully tasted warm bread and sweet wine in His mouth, traced patterns in the sand with His fingertip, brushed swaying tips of grain as He walked through sunny fields, and knelt in grassy gardens beneath dewy stars and olive trees.

The Creator became an awestruck creature. And no blade of grass, no pebble, bud, or grain of sand, no cub or sparrow or human being was left unloved.

The secret years of Christ were neither specifically for His public ministry nor for the record of sacred books. They were for *Him*. The hidden years were for His human body and human soul, for His senses, imagination, memory, and delight. And for His sacrifice.

The blood He poured forth from His Sacred Heart upon the Cross was the blood of a *man*, who lived, who loved, who knew the exquisite beauty and innocent joy of being human — body and soul.

Through divine love in the Paschal Mystery — the life, death, Resurrection, and Ascension of the Son of God — Jesus Christ assumes every aspect of being purely human and divinely transcends time and space, living eternally present, eternally *Himself*, then, now, and forever.

So it is that the Christ Child Himself crunches leaves in my wheelchair on an autumn afternoon, when our hearts beat as one in the sacred wonder of our shared humanity and the divine grace of ever-present love.

How blessed it is — the blessed privilege of sanctified and redeemed human beings — to live our lives with complete faith in God's goodness, freely traveling the paths of earthly marvels, with hearts full of childlike wonder. May we all, as little children, trust in God's ways, seeking the heavenly joy in God's Creation as Jesus does with, in, and through us.

This Is My Beloved

On the Revelation of Identity:
Christ's Baptism, Temptation in the
Wilderness, and First Miracle,
Introduced by My Parents' Discovery

Finding Out about Christina

There is a time in my family history that my mother refers to as "when we found out about Christina." No, it's not when she discovered that she was pregnant with me or even when I was born. It's when she and my father received the news of my diagnosis.

I had been such a healthy-seeming baby, with just the right amount of chubbiness, a clever, laughing, and smiling infant, who was both self-entertaining and interactive. Then my mother noticed that my legs were floppy, and my knees didn't lock when I was held in a standing position. She brought these facts to the doctor's attention on my nine-month checkup, and he agreed that there was something *different* about me. That's when the questions and searching began.

There was obviously some kind of abnormality, a secret within my flesh, a hidden truth that needed to be revealed. My body was penetrated by X-rays, needles, and electric currents, probing for answers. My deep secret was sought by pulling fluid from my veins and spine, and finally, by surgically slicing off a piece of muscle.

And then they knew. They uncovered my true identity.

I was not a healthy baby. I had Spinal Muscular Atrophy.

My mother and father were both carriers of this rare and incurable disease, and they didn't even know it.

The neurologist sat down with my parents and told them what had been discovered about their daughter. They were told that their baby with the big eyes and ready smile, their bright and happy child, was never going to walk, that she would always be crippled. The muscles of her body would become progressively weaker, collapsing her spine in scoliosis and compromising her lungs. She would develop serious pneumonia, Dr. Norgren informed them. And before the age of thirteen, their little girl would die. "But," he said as a kind of consolation, "she will always have her smile."

The revelation of my disease was a shock to my parents, as it would be to anyone.

Although the doctors were wrong about my lifespan, they were right about pretty much everything else. I never walked, never toileted myself, and every year I got weaker and weaker. I never became physically independent. The dependency and weakening are still continuing, decades later, but so is my life.

So, what did my parents actually find out about Christina, about *me*, all of those years ago? They found out about my inabilities. They discovered that my strength would never increase. Rather, it would decrease. They learned that my everyday survival would always be fragile and dependent on others. They found out that their lives as parents would be vastly different from what they had planned and that many of the dreams that they had for me would never come true.

Everyday life had not armed them for this altered life. They weren't prepared to receive this radical change in who they thought I was. They were unprepared in every way, except one: love. They were well-equipped with real love. Their loving of me, therefore, did not change, even if their caring for me did.

Of course, my parents had already known "Christina"; they had known my identity: I was their daughter, a gift from God.

On that day of diagnosis, however, this knowledge, this identity, had temporarily become an uncertainty. What had been revealed to them was a radical departure from normalcy. As they thought about the difficulties and sacrifices ahead and the sorrows that I would surely suffer under the burden of my disease, it was a challenge for them to fully embrace my new life. Because my disease is genetic, my mother even thought that I would blame them and hate them for ever having conceived me.

Clearly, what my parents did *not* find out about me on that day was that I would never be angry at them for bringing me into the world. No. Rather, I am grateful every day that they did! Disease or no disease, I have always been glad to be alive. Dr. Norgren had been right about my smile — with my facial muscles unaffected by SMA, I've been able to retain my *ability* to smile. More importantly, I have also kept my *capacity* for smiling, for joy. Even through the struggles and tears of my childhood, the full truth of who I am as a human being on Earth was slowly revealed to my parents. They discovered that I would always be their bright and joyful daughter, loving them, loving life.

My parents gradually found out something about themselves, too. The momentous day of my diagnosis was also the first day that they began to discover their own deep strengths and unique gifts. They possess understanding, acceptance, patience, selflessness, generosity, and undaunted joy — strengths and gifts which were not readily apparent in their grieving, but which slowly unfurled within them. Love was the key that opened their hearts to divine grace, so that they could recognize the truth, beauty, and goodness of self-sacrificing love and be fulfilled in who they were created to be. Love was the key that opened their eyes, so that they could see the truth about themselves, their children, and the terribly beautiful and sacred wonder of human life.

It's Good to Be Here

It's true that I am a different kind of person than the one my parents had originally perceived me to be. My life is different than the life that they had envisioned for me, and what's abnormal about me brings adversities — there's no sugarcoating that. But the truth of who I am is the same as it ever was and ever will be: I am a divinely treasured creation, a simply complex human being, a beloved child of God — and of Dan and Francine.

Unrecognized

"There is one among you who you do not recognize."[12]

Mine is a little life. Unable to be employed, get married, be a mother, or leave my house often, my circle of acquaintances is extraordinarily limited. The majority of people in my hometown don't even know that I exist, but that's actually a rather common thing. Most of us live in obscurity, unknown to the world. In our modern society, more and more people seem to be getting individually noticed through social media, as in videos that go viral or stories that tell of their sensational deeds, whether good or bad. This kind of recognition is short-lived, however, and doesn't reveal the fullness of the person's personality or life. Who really knows who we are? Most of us are not even known by name outside of our families, friends, and circles of people within our communities, like neighbors, classmates, coworkers, or health care givers.

This is normal in a wholesome way, keeping with the divine order of earthly life. The point of living as a human being is not to make oneself known to the masses. It is to *love*. And whether or not we are recognized for this love, for our goodness and charity, is

[12] John 1:26.

ultimately unimportant, because our every act of love is seen and celebrated by the One who knows us better than we even know ourselves, by the One who is the Creator and Master of all: God.

This littleness of human life is what God chose to live Himself. Fully divine though Jesus was, He was nonetheless raised in a small, backwater town by a construction worker and a housewife, poor by many standards and unknown in wider circles. Ordinary was He. For thirty years, multitudes of His fellow human beings passed Him by without the slightest idea that He was God living among them. People would have looked right at Him and seen only a nice little boy or a diligent young man. Most people would have looked right at Him and looked right *through* Him, not even seeing or thinking about Him at all, as so many of us do when we pass strangers on the street or in the aisles of church. If we had been alive in the first century and had accidentally bumped into Jesus, chances are that we wouldn't have recognized Him as anyone different or special and would have moved on past the guy without a second thought.

That's the way God wanted it. That was the divine plan, so that Jesus was able to live His life on Earth in normal obscurity. Only the people directly in His life knew Him by name, and they saw Him as the grown-up He had become: a good man who had learned the construction trade from His foster father and was living with His widowed mother. And then ... and then came the day when this man transcended His ordinary life.

He was baptized.

John, a member of Jesus's extended family, was a man who lived differently, a man who stood out, wearing wild clothes, living in the desert on wild honey and locusts, and preaching a baptism of water for the forgiveness of sins. Although he wasn't exactly like the man on the street corner yelling, "The end is near!" he was pretty close. "Metanoia! Repent and change!" he said. "The kingdom of God is at hand!"[13] We can well imagine that most people dismissed John and passed him by with a shake of the head. There were some, however, who knew that they needed to change, that the lives that they were living were not in accord with the ways of God, and they wanted to be converted. They listened to this extraordinary man and repented of their wrongdoings, seeking forgiveness from God and a fresh new start as they acknowledged their sins and were immersed (baptized) by John in the River Jordan.

Some even thought that John was the promised Messiah, come to bring God's kingdom to Earth, but John told them that he was not the Holy Anointed One of God: "I baptize with water; but there is one among you whom you do not recognize, the one who is coming after me, whose sandal strap I am not worthy to untie."[14] John further said, "I have baptized you with water; he will baptize you with the holy Spirit."[15]

Then Jesus came to the banks of the River Jordan. He didn't stand out; He was just another man in the crowd who stepped forward for His turn to be baptized by John, but John did not want to baptize Him as he had been baptizing others. He knew Jesus's secret, recognizing that Jesus was wholly different. John knew that Jesus didn't have any sins to acknowledge or any need for forgiveness. Jesus, however, insisted on receiving John's baptism in order "to fulfill all righteousness"[16]— in order to fulfill God's plan for humankind.

---

[13] Matthew 3:2.
[14] John 1:26–27.
[15] Mark 1:8.
[16] Matthew 3:15.

God became human in order to unite divinity with humanity, and humanity with divinity. And when Jesus was baptized in the River Jordan, He was fully identifying Himself with humankind, showing Himself to be fully human by letting Himself be submerged beneath the water like all of those who did so before Him and who did so after Him. Although not a sinner Himself, He submitted to the baptism of sinners, stooping low, holding His breath as John pushed Him below the river's surface, feeling the cool current flow all along His skin, opening His eyes for a moment to see the sky above distorted through the water. And then He stood, rising up to inhale deeply and shake the dripping wetness out of His hair and off of His drenched body.

Fully human, Christ was baptized by John. Then, on rising up out of the waters, Christ Jesus was identified as fully divine as the heavens tore open, the Holy Spirit descended on Him like a dove, and the heavenly voice declared, "This is my beloved Son."[17]

In one sense, the baptism of Jesus in the Jordan was like those of all of the other people baptized by John — it signified a new beginning. His fellow human beings around Him, having repented of their sins, pledged to go forward and live new lives devoted to love of God and neighbor. Jesus, though He had no sins of which to repent and no need to rededicate Himself to holiness, did also go forward from the banks of the Jordan to live in a different way. He would no longer remain in anonymity. Starting with His baptism, the fullness of who He was began to be revealed. Jesus's life changed in the sense that He started to actively and publicly live the entirety of His identity as both human *and* divine.

[17] Matthew 3:17.

Through Christ's life, including His teaching, healing, suffering, death, Resurrection, and Ascension, a new life has been made available to every human being, to each and every one of us. When we receive Jesus's Baptism, through His Church, we don't merely receive a symbolic new start, as those who were baptized by John. Rather, we are sacramentally baptized into Jesus's divine life, into the full reality of His life, death, Resurrection, and Ascension—we are made into new creations. We are no longer ordinary. Though we may still live in human obscurity, unrecognized by the masses, we are recognized, as always, by God as His beloved sons and daughters, and we are restored to divine image and likeness *through* Christ. Our souls are indelibly changed, the crippling shackles of original sin cut free from us, and we are given divine gifts so that we may no longer be obscured by sin but may cooperate with grace and be resplendent in God's glory.

We are called to live this holy, extraordinary life in simple and ordinary ways. Our missions won't necessarily be to do great things that will bring us worldly recognition but rather, as St. Teresa of Calcutta has said, to do little things, even things unnoticed by the world, with great love. Our lives may be little, but great is God's love for us. That's the love that we are meant to live, now and forever.

You, my fellow Christian, are bathed in the glory of God because you have been baptized in the name of the Father, and of the Son, and of the Holy Spirit. You are adopted into the divine Sonship of Christ and have become His beloved sibling. You are holy and new. This is your true identity. Live your baptismal promise to break away from the self-centeredness of sin, and live in the extraordinary love of God!

The next time that you gather with others for worship, look to your left, and look to your right. See the petulant and whining child, the crumpled elderly person who smells like urine, the young woman on the smartphone, the young man with the tattoos, and remember who they are. Do not let appearances or current choices obscure your vision so that they go unrecognized by you. Recognize them as fellow sons and daughters of God Most High.

Into the Desert

If you were God come down to live on Earth for a time, what would you do?

Would you let yourself suffer hunger? Would you submit to mere mortals' teachings and household rules? Would you submit to being a servant of another and even wash people's feet? Would you let yourself be wrongly arrested, tortured, and killed? Such things do not seem godly. We might perceive such experiences as signs of weakness and as downright demeaning, ones we would avoid if we had the power of God. For God would never let Himself suffer the way so many of us human beings do. Surely not.

And yet, He did.

God Incarnate was carried in the womb of His mother for nine months, born in a stable, raised in obscurity without luxury, and worked hard for a living. After living a very ordinary and commonplace existence, Jesus was revealed as God's beloved Son at His baptism in the River Jordan. With His divine Sonship made manifest to those who listened, Jesus did not then proceed to live a rich, prestigious, and lordly life. Instead, He was immediately led by the Spirit into the desert to fast for forty days. There, in the wilderness, Jesus, fully divine and fully human, was further subjected to the struggles of all of humankind by experiencing our very human desires, enticed to serve His human will rather than divine will. Further confirming the bond of the divine and human, He, who is without sin, was Himself tempted by the urges that are due to our sinfulness. Jesus did not give into these temptations, these desires of the flesh, but He did experience them. That's what the temptations in the wilderness were for—to unite divinity ever more completely with every struggling human being in this fallen world and so draw us more deeply into God's love. To that end, He was spared nothing.

Christ chose to fast for forty days and forty nights, becoming hungry, perhaps a little delirious, and suffering the lures of the spiritual adversary, called Satan, who strives to divert each and every human being away from loving God. It was not solely Jesus's *human* will to fast—God chose to do this. It was Jesus's divine choice to endure human sufferings and cravings, and it was the divine Spirit that led Him. Soon enough, there in the wilderness, the lack of food started to get to His human nature.

Being fully human, Jesus was naturally hungry. Very, very hungry. His body wanted food. Being also fully divine, why didn't Jesus simply turn the stones into bread to eat? That's the question the adversary put to Him.

God knows that there is *real* hunger in the world, terribly worse than ordinary pangs in the middle of the night or after working hard. His Chosen People suffered hunger in the desert during their exodus from Egypt, and Christ identified with them when He, too, was hungry in the desert. But God also sees the parents who go without food so that their children won't go to bed hungry; the people who die from malnutrition and starvation every day because of famine; and the neglected elderly and disabled people, who cannot speak for themselves or feed themselves, and who are wasting away, starving, abandoned in corners. God has compassion on each and every one of them, uniting Himself *in the flesh* with the suffering hungry. By so doing, God sanctifies them, giving them Himself in the unfathomable gift of divine solidarity.

Jesus chose not to turn stones into bread when He was hungry in the desert because *we* don't have the power to do that when *we* are hungry. It is God the Father's will for the Son, who is fully God, to become human and to suffer with us in divine love. Christ is like us in all ways but sin. He remained true to living as a limited human like us in the midst of His own suffering, keeping to the divine plan. And by keeping unwaveringly to the divine plan, He remained free of sin.

By declaring to the tempter, "One does not live by bread alone, but by every word that comes forth from the mouth of God,"[18] Jesus not only reminded all of us what (or rather, *Who*) the ultimate source and sustenance of our lives is, but He also rationally encouraged His human flesh to stay firm in divine will.

Then and now, Christ is truly with us, in all of our struggles, *struggling with us.*

The spiritual adversary, the evil one, continued to try to pry Jesus away from divine will — because that's what Satan does to human beings. In the second temptation in the desert, Jesus basically got dared. He was taken to a great height where Satan said, "If you are the Son of God, throw yourself down,"[19] implying, "Being who You are, nothing bad will happen to You." We can imagine how tempting that would be.

Being fully human, Jesus might have listened, wishing, like us, to test and see, without relying solely on faith (and while

[18] Matthew 4:4.
[19] Matthew 4:6.

He was at it, enjoy the thrill of extreme sports in the free fall). Being also fully divine, why didn't He let the angels catch Him mid-plunge as He knew that they would?

Like any good and faithful human being, Jesus knew that He was not on Earth for the sake of His own finite whims and pleasures. He lived on Earth as proof that success in life is not defined by being able to do whatever you want without consequences, and that there is more to life than the thrills of a moment, more to life than what we can physically do or not do. Love, the authentic gift of oneself to another that requires sacrifice, is what life is about. Love is the source of real joy—a truth, not a theory, that Jesus fully embraced. "You shall not put the Lord, your God, to the test,"[20] He said.

For the final temptation, Satan turned to the human urge for power, the motivation of greed. He showed Jesus all of the human kingdoms with their splendor and majesty and said, "All these I shall give to you, if you will prostrate yourself and worship me."[21] Being fully human, Jesus was tempted to serve only His appetites, to give into the call of Satan to turn away from the demands of serving His fellow human beings. Being also fully divine, why didn't He change the plan of salvation and indulge in the fleshly pleasures of His created world?

The adversary does not want humankind to be elevated through the Incarnation. The evil one thinks that it's beneath even the angels to serve human beings. Monstrous to Satan, then, is the thought of God Himself becoming a human being to *suffer* as a human being for the sake of human beings. Jesus even referred to Simon Peter as Satan when this loving disciple

[20] Matthew 4:7.
[21] Matthew 4:9.

declared that Jesus, the Christ, should not have to suffer a torturous and humiliating death. "Get behind me, Satan!"[22] He said to His friend. And in Christ's last admonition to the devil in the desert, He says:

> Get away, Satan! It is written:
> "The Lord, your God, shall you worship
> and him alone shall you serve."[23]

Jesus freely, completely, and most willingly chose love of others over any self-centered desire. With that, His struggle with temptation was completed.

Goaded in the desert, what Jesus experienced was the temptation of every human from the beginning of humankind, the temptation that *we* face every day. Whom shall we serve? Do we choose to love ourselves, our earthly, finite, limited selves over God? Or do we choose to love God, infinite and eternal, over our finite selves? Our everyday temptations may seem small in comparison to those of Christ. Tempting questions we hear may be more like: Why don't I lie to get more sympathy? Why don't I ignore my friend when I feel like it, knowing that she'll come back later? Why don't I belittle this person with whom I am arguing? These lures are as much a part of being human as Christ's temptations are. His were more pointed in their direct disobedience to God, their direct rejection of God's will, but that's because He is without sin.

The temptation of Christ is the temptation of a human being who did not inherit the stain of original sin, with darkened intellect and weakened will. The first humans, called Adam and

---

[22] Matthew 16:23.
[23] Matthew 4:10.

Eve in the Bible, started off *innocent*. Although they were not divine, they experienced spiritual familiarity with God, walking and talking with God in paradise. Despite this closeness, they were tempted by selfish pride. The choice confronted them: would they live self-centered or God-centered lives?

They chose poorly.

The Virgin Mary, too, was innocent. Created by God to be His mother, she was different than the rest of us, being kept free from the rift between God and man, the rift caused by the first humans' choosing of the finite over the infinite, which is the origin of all sin. Therefore, she was like Adam and Eve before their fall, so that she could be the "New Eve" as part of God's plan of salvation to redeem humankind. When the angel Gabriel declared God's will to her, for her to become pregnant by the Holy Spirit, a plan that risked her being stoned as an adulteress, she had the same ageless question placed before her. Would she choose what may have seemed right and good for her material life, serving her finite self over God? Or would she choose faith in God's will, trusting, loving, and serving God over her finite concerns, giving herself completely to love?

She chose wisely.

Christ chose wisely, too. He is, after all, God.

We think that being God would be like being human with limitless power, but that just shows how limited our understanding is and how far our ways are from God's ways. We would like God's power over matter, forgetting about the *most powerful force of all*, the one that God has in infinite abundance because it is precisely what God is: *love*. God's power of love drove Jesus into the desert. Love for God the Father — and love for us.

When we have this understanding, the results of the desert temptations may seem to have been a forgone conclusion, hardly worth undergoing. However, what Jesus went through in the wilderness is what gives us this understanding of what it means to be God.

And what it means to be human.

Human life is not without struggle and hardship. The perfect human being—God in the flesh—did not use divine power to overcome struggle or avoid hardship. He used divine power so that He could suffer, too, and, by so suffering, be able to love in the most profoundly complete and unimaginably powerful way possible: not only as God, but also as man. Christ's very real temptations and struggles are cosmically important because, by going through them, Christ *sanctifies* the battles within each and every one of us, proving that they are not obstacles to our joy as fulfilled persons. Our natural limitations are sacred, because *the full reality of being human* is sacred. We are walking with Christ, we are living divine lives, *even when we are tempted,* so long as, in our reactions and decisions, we trust God and remain lovingly with Christ, striving to choose wisely. As we persevere in choosing love and holiness, Christ is with us—even when we fail, as long as we fervently try—over and over again.

In the Beginning

When we think of living divine lives in a sanctified place, we may think of a world with no imperfections, no bodily ailments or mental illnesses, no diseases, disabilities, or deformities. No suffering. However, that is not the definition of a sanctified place, of a holy place in which God dwells.

For Christ dwelt *here*.

God Incarnate lived in the world, in this very imperfect, frail, and suffering world. It didn't need to be rendered flawless in order for Him to make it His home, and suffering did not melt away in His presence, even though He cured many afflictions.

In fact, the first miracle in St. John's Gospel is not a cure. Of all the tremendous and fantastic things that Christ could have done in the beginning of His public ministry, He chose to resupply alcohol at a party. Specifically, He miraculously changed water into wine at a wedding reception.

Why?

A marriage is a beautiful and holy thing, a bit of Heaven on Earth — the elevation of the human to the divine and the consecration of the divine in the human. That is why Christ, one of many invited guests, chose a celebration of marriage for the performance of His first miracle. He wanted to begin the manifestation of His divine power on Earth with *the beginning*.

Marrying

In the beginning God created the heavens and the earth. And the earth was without form, and void; and darkness was upon the face of the deep. And the Spirit of God moved upon the face of the waters.[24]

By the will of God, the universe was created. God's Spirit moved upon the face of the dark abyss, and God's Word called forth light, form, and life. All that God creates is good. God wills that it should be so. By the will of God, we human beings exist, created in divine image and likeness by the Word of God, male and female, with life breathed into us by the Spirit of God. Human life is good, very good.

Because man is created in the image and likeness of God, it was not good for man to be solitary. Although God is *one* divine Being, He is not solitary, in that God exists mysteriously as a communion of the divine Persons we know as Father, Son, and Holy Spirit. The Holy Trinity may be too mysterious for us to comprehend, but we *are* able to understand that *love* cannot be solitary. Love *must* be given and received. So, because we know that God is love — always has been and always will be — we know that God must have always been able to give and receive love, to give and receive Himself, and therefore cannot be solitary, cannot be alone. To be truly in the image of God, therefore, man must be able to freely give and receive love. Man's primary relationship is,

[24] Genesis 1:1–2 (KJV).

and always will be, with God, with the triune majesty of divine persons, but man must also be able to give and receive love to and from an equal, in communion with *human* persons.

Therefore, God created man in His divine image: *male and female* God created them. When a male human and a female human come together in true marriage, they image both the unitive and creative powers of God.

At a wedding, the man and woman freely give themselves to each other in love, a blessed union of persons, reflecting the union of three divine Persons in one God, who is love itself. This union of two human beings has the power to bring forth new persons into the world, a cooperation and participation in the creative power of God, which allows you and me to be here. Each and every human being is sacred, as is the way in which they come into existence: the joining, the marrying, of a man and a woman. A wedding celebration, therefore, is a holy celebration of both love *and* life—a celebration of the sacred wonder of humankind, created in the image of God.

A true marriage is a taste of Eden before it was corrupted by pride and lust.

With this knowledge of marriage, Christ celebrated with His neighbors, friends, and family in Cana and sanctified the rite with His first miracle.

The Natural and the Supernatural

The miracle at the wedding feast in Cana is the realization of God in both Creation and human love. Jesus didn't need to provide more wine because the hosts ran out of it. His mother simply asked Him to do something for the people, to help them. Being a dutiful and respectful Son, *fully human*, He honored His mother's request. He didn't do this by giving them money from His wallet to buy more wine or by getting a collection together for a run to the local store. Rather, Jesus fulfilled His mother's request by performing a miracle, as only God can. Harkening back to the Creation story in the book of Genesis, the Spirit of God moved upon the waters in the jars, and Christ brought forth wonderfully delicious wine from the deep. Jesus, *fully divine*, has power over the created order.

The *naturally* produced wine at the celebration was good, and Jesus, His mother, and His disciples drank it, but they did not overindulge. Those who did not fall to self-indulgence were then able to fully taste and experience the superior goodness of the *supernaturally* procured wine. On the other hand, those who were drunk would have been oblivious to the fruits of God's presence among them. Just so, those who do not self-centeredly overindulge in earthly pleasures, including the pleasures of marriage, leave room for God. They live fully as God-centered human beings upon the earth, enjoying the goodness and the wonder of being alive, flesh and spirit, in God's beautiful Creation, while remaining open to experiencing and enjoying something even more amazing—the infinite joy of the divine way *within* our earthly lives.

Performing this specific miracle at a specific wedding puts into action, in a particular and very human way, the mission for which God came to live among us, Christ's reason for being: to restore humankind to divine image and to reopen paradise for us as our eternal way of life. Cana becomes a new Eden for a moment, as we are again reminded that God looked upon all that He had created—the waters that rain and flow in streams, the plants of the earth, the fruit of the vine, the creatures of both flesh and spirit, the love and life that comes from their union—and God saw that it was *good*.

3

If You Will It, Lord

*On Suffering and True Healing:
Miracles from the Bible, Christ's Regard
for the Poor, and Prayer's Answer,
Introduced by My Understanding of
Disease and Divine Love*

Imperfect

The woman in church bent down beside me in my wheelchair, her hands clasped at her knees, and looked tenderly into my eyes. "You are one of God's special children," she said to me, "and He loves you very much." I was inexperienced in the ways of faith, and I didn't understand the profound power of the words "He loves you." So, as a teenager who was not yet a true Christian, I may have smirked a bit at the woman's message. I did not, however, tell her what I was thinking: that being in a wheelchair didn't make me special, and I didn't need to be patronized. My self-esteem was high, so I knew that I was lovable and unique, but for reasons other than the faulty gene that I happened to have inherited.

This kind of situation has been common in my life. I have been told by others that my disability is evidence that God loves me especially, as if God loves me so much that He gave me a disabling disease in order for me to be closer to Him. This idea was never expressed to me by any of my close family members, so it was not ingrained in my brain. Rather, the concept came to me from near strangers, like well-meaning people at church. So, as an external concept, I could analyze it with detachment, and I have always found it difficult to believe as true. I wondered, "Is that how God really works? Choosing favorites and giving extra hardships to them?" I sure hoped not. That didn't sound like a loving God.

Now, as a grown-up and committed Christian, I understand how hardship in this life can deepen a person's heart and may cause that person to develop a closer relationship with Infinite and Eternal God, but this deepened heart and relationship is not a guaranteed result of suffering. And I still do not believe that God *gave* me my disabling disease or that He would do so because He loves me as one of His special children. This is not how I understand disease *or* God's love.

It seems to me that the physical world in which we live is simply limited. Creation itself, though it comes from God, is not God—and only God is perfect. Therefore, Creation and all creatures within it are not perfect. The universe unfolds with rich multiplicity through ebb and flow, fire and ice, the making and breaking of molecular bonds, and the division and diversification of cells. The beautiful complexity and variety of the created world comes through fractures, lapses, and compensations. Hence, one little gene responsible for the survival of motor nerve cells mutates, and some babies, like me, are never able to walk.

This is a great sadness. Disease is a hard and undesirable part of life. I have never wanted to be disabled. I still don't want to be, but I understand that we humans are imperfect creatures, susceptible to flaw and failure. Because of the first humans' failures in trust and love, putting their finite selves ahead of infinite God, we have put things out of order. We have fallen away from the full goodness of living centered in God. And because we no longer live in a paradisiacal state of trusting and loving union with the Divine, the imperfections of the natural world have become overwhelming ordeals. Through our fall from grace, with weakened will and darkened intellect, serious imperfections can become terrible sufferings that they were not intended to be. All of this is compounded with the sufferings that we endure—and inflict—through cruel and selfish choices made by free will.

When God chose to come among us and walk upon Earth, He did not avoid suffering. God did not consider human dependency and helplessness to be beneath Him, but rather, He embraced it and assumed it for Himself. God Incarnate lived the limitations and vulnerability of infancy, as well as the pangs of hunger and thirst, and the sweat and ache of fatigue.

God willingly entered into suffering, experiencing the scourge of cruelty, the torture of evil intentions, betrayal, grief, and dread. He endured profound suffering, agony, *immobility*, and pain. God even tasted death.

This is what God did because He loves me! God didn't give me suffering out of His great love for me. Rather, God took my suffering onto *Himself* out of that great love.

The fallen world in which we live is a world of sorrow, affliction, and pain. God knows. But God loves us so much that He won't let us suffer alone. He doesn't expect us to go through anything that He isn't willing to go through Himself. Christ, God in the flesh, didn't have to suffer—He *chose* to, so that He could be with us in our every anguish and tribulation. Now, whenever we suffer, whenever we experience the misery of sickness or the torment of a loved one's illness, we are with Christ, as He is with us.

Does God's decision to suffer with us mean that we shouldn't work to alleviate suffering when we can? No. We are called to have the compassion and courage to change the things that we can in order to reduce suffering in people's lives, with loving concern for the *whole* well-being of *every* human being, now and forever. That's what love is for, as my parents have shown me in their generous caring for me. Our enduring fulfillment as divine images is in self-giving, sacrificing, love.

Does God's choice to sacrifice Himself to endure our pain with us make pain less than pain? No. Pain is pain. And yet ...

If I offer up my pain for Christ, united with Christ's offering up of His life for me on the Cross, then I can allow myself to know something of the profound compassion that Christ Crucified has for me. If, while wanting a little pity for myself, I can, in my suffering, take pity on Jesus *in His*, then He will open my mind and heart to His endless strength and peace. If I suffer *for love* of God, as God willingly suffers for love of me, then my soul can breathe freely *through* the suffering, and I can know that I am not full of *pain*. I am full of *love*.

In faith, trust, and courage, we must reach out to Christ in our sufferings, and touching the Cross, the intersection of the human and the divine where Christ hangs in agony, we will be suspended with Him and filled with the power of His love. Receiving that love that God freely gives to us, allowing divine love to fill us, we can then be healed of the divisions that keep us from knowing joy, and we can freely and lovingly give ourselves to God.

For what purpose is an offering of pain to Christ? God knows. Perhaps only God knows, but since we will one day know fully, as we are fully known by God,[25] then we will surely know in time. Beyond time. What we can know now, in part, in current time and space, through faith and hope, is that Christ's pain brings healing and restoration to humankind — it brings

---

[25] 1 Corinthians 13:12.

salvation. When we give our pain to Christ, uniting our suffering with His, then He allows our pain to mysteriously bring salvation, too.

God entered into our suffering in order to transform the meaning of suffering, using suffering itself as the means of our ultimate healing.[26] This concept is profoundly mysterious but not unfamiliar. In the natural world, we can see how God allows less than desirable workings to bring about beauty in the finite ways of Creation. Through arduous labor, new life is born into the world. Through the eruption of volcanoes, lush, green islands are formed. Through the decomposition of furry little creatures into the forest floor, majestic trees are fed to provide a sanctuary of life. Tears of rain water the roses, while fallen acorns sustain the squirrels. Who am I to question the wisdom of autumn beauty, with its dying leaves of brilliant splendor, or the necessity of planet-breaking shooting stars? We may not like the fact that the world in which we live is structured by circles of destruction, but that's how it is. And our merciful God makes all things work for good for those who love Him.[27]

Jesus says to us, "In the world you have tribulation; but be of good cheer, I have overcome the world."[28]

With faith and growing understanding, I would like to respond to the woman in church and to all of the others who think of me as especially loved because of my disease. I would like to tell them that God loves me because that's what God *does*—because that's *who* God *is*. I want them to know that they are special,

---

[26] See Peter Kreeft, *Because God Is Real: Sixteen Questions, One Answer* (San Francisco: Ignatius Press, 2008), Q. 15.

[27] Romans 8:28.

[28] John 16:33 (RSV).

beloved children of God, too, fearfully and wonderfully made with unique gifts to offer.

Every human being is particularly loved by God, no matter what.

God made us to be human. And to be human is to be limited. And to be limited, here and now, is to be wanting. And to be wanting is to be seeking. To be seeking is to be willing. To be willing is to be open. To be open is to be awed. To be awed is to be redeemed. To be redeemed is to be fulfilled. And to be fulfilled is to be full of divine love.

To be full of divine love is to be joyful.

God is whom I want and seek; God's way is what I will. God opens me, and it is by and through Him that I am awed and redeemed. God made me for love, and I am unfulfilled until I rest fully in Him who is Love.[29]

Here and now, everybody is limited. Everybody is flawed. God didn't make us to be flawed; God made us to be *loved*. The evidence that I am a special child of God, beloved by God, is that I am *a human being*—made for divine love, made for infinite joy. Just like everybody. Just like *you*.

[29] See St. Augustine, *Confessions*, bk. 10.

Why Are You Thinking Such Things in Your Heart?

As a person with a disability, I think with particular interest on how Jesus, who is God Incarnate, treated the disabled during His earthly life. We know that He cured many. In fact, He gained notoriety as a healer, going about giving sight to the blind, hearing to the deaf, and the ability to walk to the crippled—all things that the prophet Isaiah foretold about the Messiah.

From this, we might conclude that what God wants to bring to us is the healthy functioning of brain and body. We may think that the divine ideal of a human being who walks with Christ is one of perfect physical and mental soundness. We may even believe that true peace, justice, and happiness can only be experienced on Earth when there are no infirmities or detriments of physical and mental ability. Such a conclusion may then lead us to think that the highest aim and ideal of humankind is to eradicate disease—so much so, that we might even start thinking in terms of eradicating diseased people themselves, through abortion, euthanasia, physician-assisted suicide, or embryonic destruction.

That's the kind of thinking that I'm witnessing in the world today, but it's a false understanding of God's ideal, of Jesus's purpose as a healer, of the sanctity of the human body, of the worthiness of life, and of the profound reason for the Incarnation itself.

The Gospel of St. Matthew doesn't even record the physical miracles of Jesus until chapter eight, focusing, rather, on His holiness, His teaching, His call for repentance, and His invitation to return to God. What's first and foremost is Christ's living and delivering of the Word of God, for He is the Word of God made flesh. In telling the story of Jesus Christ, none of the Gospel writers begin with His miracles of physical healing. It's almost as if those miraculous cures just naturally came about along the way.

It would be natural that God Incarnate, while He walked upon Earth, would, with a fully human sense of pity, relieve the suffering of His beloved creatures as He passed by. He was a kindhearted man and did not need to say no to His fellow humans who were directly asking for cures. However, this is not the *reason* that God became incarnate. If the key to true human joy was physical and mental soundness, then miraculous cures would happen for every believer.

But they don't.

Why?

God is love and wants us to be joyful. God knows that illness and disability do not block our ability to be truly and fully joyful because our true and complete joy comes from living in harmony with divine love, in truly *giving and receiving* love. Receiving and giving God's love is the key to true happiness. Sadly, we too often don't live this way, and, able-bodied or not, we suffer because of it. We are blind and deaf to God's love for each and every one of us, and we are unable to walk in the ways of faith, peace, and love for one another.

Our inability to live in harmony with divine will and our lack of truly loving one another—this is the suffering that God came to heal.

The worst thing that can befall a human being is not sickness or disability. We have a hard time understanding this when we think only in terms of the flesh and not the spirit, when we see things only with our limited eyes instead of striving to look at things through the eyes of faith. Without looking with the spiritual eyes of faith, we cannot see the way that God sees; we cannot see the fullness of truth. The truth is that there is nothing about being chronically or terminally ill, about being blind, deaf, or mute, or about having impairments in cognition or mobility that disable us from receiving God's love and loving to the best of our abilities. *This love* is the joyful fulfillment of being human.

Throughout human history, including Jesus's time on Earth, people have not thought about illness or disability in this way. People thought that the cause of infirmities was sin. (Some people still think that.) People who were struck down by injury or illness, the thought went, were stuck down as punishment by God—like they did something to deserve it. Similarly, people who were born with a disease or birth defect were often thought of as being punished by God for the sins of their parents or community. With this kind of thinking, people who were less than healthy were looked upon as cursed in a way, lacking divine favor, as if God was withholding His love and blessing from them.

Christ proved to us that this simply isn't true.

The man who was born blind must have had sinned himself or had parents who sinned, so everybody thought. But Jesus negated that notion. Jesus told His disciples that sin was not associated with blindness. In fact, the man's blindness would be an opportunity "so that the works of God might be made visible."[30] When Jesus cured the man, the Pharisees and others were incredulous as to what had occurred. There was much back-and-forth between the man, the neighbors, the man's parents, and the Pharisees because the Pharisees didn't seem to want to listen to the previously blind man when he himself told them what had happened and who had cured him. In their blinded eyes, blinded to the Light of the World, the man born without visual sight had been born in sin and *had nothing of value to say.*

People who think that way are the ones with the true sin and are most pitiably blind.

Since the thought of Jesus's day was that people with disabilities or diseases were wicked, unclean, and unfit for worship, they were barred from holy places. By showing great mercy toward the physically and mentally afflicted in His historical time, even physically touching those deemed untouchable,[31] Jesus shows that every human being should be respected as a child of God, with the freedom to worship, and should be given compassionate care. Through His many healings and parables, like that of the Good Samaritan,[32] Jesus shows the people of Israel — and all of us — what true sin is. Sin is selfishness, shown in the deficiency of mercy and caring for those who suffer and in the arrogance of thinking of ourselves as superior. All sins stem from a lack of willingness to give ourselves in true love — to love God first and foremost, the ever-loving giver of life, and to genuinely love ourselves and all humans as images of God.

[30] John 9:3.
[31] See Mark 1:40–42.
[32] See Luke 10:25–37.

To forever put an end to the notion that disability and illness only afflict the wicked and faithless and are, therefore, punishments for sin, God gives us the paralytic.[33]

Jesus was teaching and healing large groups of people in Capernaum. So many wanted to be cured by Him that they were pressing in, crowding all around Him. In order to get access to Jesus, a paralyzed man was lowered down by his friends through a hole that they had made in the roof. On seeing this man on his stretcher, so obviously in want of a bodily cure, Jesus said to him, "Child, your sins are forgiven."[34] That was it. God-made-man forgave this cripple his sins.

And he stayed paralyzed.

The most powerful thing that God can do for a human being was done for the paralyzed man: he was given the unfettered opportunity to leave behind selfishness, sinfulness, and ignorance and to live free of those chains, truly knowing and living divine love now and forever. This is what Jesus came to do. The paralytic man was very truly *healed*—but he still couldn't walk. That's because human beings can have direct contact with God, be divinely approved in their faith, and live in a full state of grace—and, yet, still lie immobile on the floor.

It was only because of the thoughts of those who considered themselves superior that Jesus turned to the physical condition of the man. The naysayers reacted to Jesus's "your sins are forgiven" by thinking that He was woefully arrogant and blasphemous in claiming that He could forgive sins, as only God could forgive sins. (Perhaps they were especially outraged that He told a disabled man, of all people, that his sins were forgiven.) Jesus

[33] See Matthew 9:1–8; Mark 2:1–12; Luke 5:17–26.
[34] Mark 2:5.

responded to their thoughts by saying, "Which is easier, to say to the paralytic, 'Your sins are forgiven,' or to say, 'Rise, pick up your mat and walk'? But that you may know that the Son of Man has authority to forgive sins on earth"—Jesus then spoke again to the man who was unable to move—"I say to you, rise, pick up your mat, and go home."[35]

With those words, the man was able to stand and walk.

Jesus did not heal the paralytic so much for the man's sake as for the sake of those who doubted Jesus's power—who didn't know who He was. Their limited brains did not deny the power of Jesus *after* the paralyzed man got up and walked, but because of their limitations, their doubts, and, yes, their sins, they could not see His divine power *before that*, when He forgave the man his sins.

Telling the paralytic to get up and walk lent authority and veracity to Jesus's first proclamation of forgiveness. The healing acted as a test to see what others would do when face-to-face with the divine power of Jesus. What was their true relationship with God? Would they run toward Him in humble acceptance, or would they run away, clinging to their own finite power, unwilling to bow before the Divine?

It was also, I think, a test to see what the people would make of this paralytic—a man whom they had identified primarily and, perhaps, solely by his disability—when he was no longer a paralytic. Who was this man to them? To Jesus, this man was exactly the same man before and after he was cured of paralysis.

The full truth of Christ's mission on Earth was not to cure every sickness, but rather to reveal divinity to humanity and to restore each of us to the fullness of God's image. Earthly life has limitations. The reason that God became one of us was not to

---

[35] Mark 2:8–11.

get rid of earthly limitations, but to bring love, *divine love*, into every situation, into every suffering.

In fact, on another occasion during which Jesus was crowded by people who wanted cures, He left without curing them. The whole town had crowded at the door of Simon and Andrew's house, but Jesus rose before dawn and went off to an isolated place to pray. Simon and his companions searched for Jesus and, when they found Him, told Him that everybody was looking for Him, implying that He should go back. He didn't. "Let us go to the nearby villages that I may preach there also," Jesus said. "For this purpose have I come."[36] Thus, Jesus left behind many who wanted to be healed of physical defects and mental afflictions — not because He didn't love them, but *because He loves us all* and ultimately strove for what is *infinitely* best for us.

The Word of God became incarnate so that we may have abundant life *in* the Word. Christ came to transform us and save us — to free us from our sins and their destructive consequences, to rescue us from the oppression of ignorant self-centeredness, and to restore us to the joyful liberation of receiving God's love and sharing that love unselfishly with others. To believe in Christ and be saved, then, is neither to be delivered from the natural limitations of being human on Earth, nor to be preserved from any bodily suffering here. It is to have our eyes and ears opened to truth, to the fullness of reality, and to have our minds and hearts healed of divisions that keep us from loving God and from loving one another. Through humble faith in Christ, then, whether or not we are able to walk with our legs, we will be able to walk gratefully with Christ in God's Way of heavenly bliss, now and forever.

---

[36] Mark 1:38.

Begging Bowls: Blessed
Are the Poor in Spirit

Who are the blessed among us? You might answer that the blessed among us are those who are most loved by God. However, God loves everybody equally because God loves infinitely. That's who God is, so that's what God does. God loves the rich and the poor, the weak and the strong, and the healthy and the sick, all with the same infinite and intimate love.

Yet knowing all of this, it does seem that Jesus, in His historical time and place, had a special kind of affection for the poor, the marginalized, the greatly suffering, and the obviously crippled. Why? Perhaps the obviously poor, outcast, and crippled were the ones who knew that they were not supremely powerful and certainly not perfect. They were the ones who knew that they were *dependent*. They were the ones who saw the truth of human life and came humbly to Jesus, empty-handed and hopeful, asking Him for divine help.

Blessed are the poor in spirit, then, because they know that they are lacking. They know that they are cripples. Fallen as we are, all human beings have been lacking the fullness of communion with God, our Creator, our Eternity. We have become disadvantaged by original sin, blinded, deafened, and impoverished—every one of us—unable to live up fully to the Divine Image in which we have been created. We live outside of paradise.

Almighty God humbly became one of us, Christ came lovingly among us, in order to fix this. But do we know that we need to be fixed? Do we know that we are in need of repair and restoration? Do we lament the divide between us and God? "Blessed are those who mourn, for they will be comforted.... Blessed are those who hunger and thirst for righteousness, for they will be satisfied."[37]

Here and now, we can be healed of our spiritual deficiencies, experience divine love, and be joyfully restored to the fullness of who we are created to be, fulfilled in eternity. Holy blessings, eternal belonging, profound goodness and joy can be ours through Christ, but only if we know that we are in need and put out our begging bowls to be filled.

[37] Matthew 5:4, 6.

Ask and You Shall Receive—Sort Of

How many people have turned away from God when their fervently prayed-for desires have not been fulfilled? How many doubt the divinity of Christ or the veracity of God's love when a cure that was prayerfully sought was not found?

I was a much-loved child. I was also, literally, a poster child for disability.

Having served as a child ambassador for my local chapter of the Muscular Dystrophy Association at the ages of six and eight, I actively represented my disabling disease at fundraisers statewide. Yet, I always felt a bit uncomfortable drumming up donations by telling people to "Help fight MD!" I had never thought of my disease as an enemy to be fought or even as something separate from myself. My disease, in my way of thinking and understanding, was simply part of me. My physical form is the way that I am, the way that I came to be. Disabled is how I live; it is the condition of my body—meaning the circumstance or shape, but also meaning that I can bodily live on Earth on one condition: I had to come here diseased, weakening every year.

Loving life and joyfully knowing that I am loved, I accepted this.

Acceptance didn't mean that I didn't want to walk and be cured of my disease. I very much wanted a cure. Living this way is frustrating, saddening, maddening, uncomfortable, exhausting, and requires much hard work and enormous sacrifice from me and the people I love. I asked God many times to grant me a miraculous cure and others have asked for me as well. Sadly, unlike many people in the New Testament, I did not receive my desired miracle.

Various possible reasons for this lack of healing were presented to me, mostly through television, but also through some well-meaning people at church, and I began to wonder if my request wasn't being granted because I was too sinful or lacking in faith. So, I tried to be good, recognizing that I wasn't as good as I could be, and I tried to have faith. I did have faith, in that I believed God had the power to wipe away my disease and disability. I would even lie in bed sometimes and pray to God, telling Him that I knew that He had the power to cure me of my disease and allow me to walk. Then, I would ask Him for that cure. In what I considered a testimony of faith, I would say, "Amen," and try to sit up and swing my feet down onto the floor, really giving it my best effort with the thought that it would work if God wanted it to work.

It didn't work. My head didn't even come off of the pillow, and my knees only leaned to the side, which was all that my body could physically accomplish. No miraculous cure.

Thankfully, this did not make me doubt God's love for me. The fact that I remained disabled did not turn me away from God for two main reasons.

The first reason was that every time I asked for a cure there was always a caveat, the caveat of Jesus Himself in His agony in the Garden of Gethsemane: "Not my will but yours be done."[38]

[38] Luke 22:42.

Like the leper that said to Jesus, "Lord, if you are willing, you can make me clean,"[39] I believed in the power of Christ to cure, but I also believed that the will of God may not be for my curing.

Thinking that God wanted to keep me disabled did not make me question the lovingness or goodness of God for another deeply important reason: I knew that I was loved. Given amazingly loving and self-sacrificing parents, a devoted sister, and a whole big, loving family, I had always known that I was loved. My God-given sense of humor and delight in simple things were appreciated and nurtured throughout my childhood, in my stable and generally happy home. People were different, and I was certainly different, often suffering because of it, but I knew that my difference was not something that had to be wiped away in order for me to be lovable and to know goodness and joy.

Yet we, as believers, recall the words of Jesus — words that cause many to wonder why prayed-for cures are not given to good people who believe in Christ. Jesus did say, "Ask and it will be given to you; seek and you will find."[40] What do we do with that?

God knows that I have asked and sought. When Jesus spoke about receiving and finding during the Sermon on the Mount, however, He concluded with this question: "Which one of you would hand his son a stone when he asks for a loaf of bread, or a snake when he asks for a fish? If you then, who are wicked, know how to give good gifts to your children, how much more will your heavenly Father give good things to those who ask him."[41]

As human beings in this fallen world, we are sinful (wicked) because of our weakened will, and we are murky in our perception

[39] Luke 5:12 (NIV).
[40] Matthew 7:7.
[41] Matthew 7:9–11.

because of our darkened intellects. In the desperation of hunger, we may, without knowing it, ask for a stone or a snake. Would God, seeing our hunger and loving us, give us precisely the thing for which we asked? Or would He give us the thing that we *need* in our hunger—the very thing that we would have asked for if we had the eyes to see and the mind to know?

As I remember, when my nephews were very young, they would sometimes ask for candy for breakfast. My sister, their mother, may have given in once or twice, but knowing that such a dose of sugar was not a good way for them to satisfy their hunger and start their day, she usually denied them. She denied them over and over. They were disappointed and maybe even a little angry with her when she didn't give them what they wanted, but in time, they came to understand. As they grew, they occasionally grabbed something sweet for themselves in the morning, but as they continued to grow, they learned that they felt better when they didn't answer this urge and, instead, ate something *better for them*.

We are God's children. We are too small to see the big picture, too limited to understand the whole of God's plan. He alone sees the eternal masterpieces that we are created to be. He gives us what is good for our glorious and eternal selves, for who we are in His divine eyes—both now and forever. In our daily sufferings, it's natural for us to ask God for relief, but in what form should that relief come? We may think that we know what is best, for we certainly know the precise thing that we *desire*. Only God knows if that precise thing truly answers our *deep* desire for joy and will be what is ultimately and eternally best for us.

God knew perfectly well that I wanted to be able to get out of bed and walk. He knew exactly why I wanted that—so that I could be free. By asking for bodily healing, however, I may have been asking for a shackle instead of a key. Maybe God didn't want me to be bound to the physical accomplishments of my temporal body and stuck on the surface of reality. Maybe He wanted to open me up to the beauty of my little life and the unique gifts that were mine to share. When I asked for a cure, what I was truly and deeply seeking was divine sanctification, *real* healing. I was disposed to receive divinely intended gifts, and God did answer my prayer. He answered my prayer for freedom by giving me the unfolding gifts of perspective and courage instead of physical health and strength, in order that I may freely choose to love—*really love*. Through the miraculous gift of God's love received, and not forsaken, I am freely and fully able to become the person I was created to be.

To *really* love, one must be willing to suffer. Loving another and wanting only easy and pleasant things to come from that loving isn't real love. Our ultimate happiness comes in *really* loving God, with all of our hearts, souls, and minds, and loving our neighbors as ourselves.[42] And if we ask for something in the *name* of Jesus, then we must ask with the *heart* of Jesus—willing to suffer for the love of God and others.

A Gospel example of getting what we need, but maybe not what we want, is the story of the wealthy young man who asked for the way to eternal life.[43] Jesus looked with love upon this young man who desired to follow Him and gave that man what he sought—but it made the man sad.

Sometimes what we receive from God makes things a little easier for us on Earth, as in the case of the many people whom Jesus cured bodily. Sometimes what we receive does not make

[42] See Luke 10:27.
[43] See Mark 10:17–27.

things easier at all. The wealthy young man was told by Jesus to sell everything that he owned and give the money to the poor. Material possessions were considered to be a great blessing in that time, as they are to most people in our own, yet Jesus told the man that, in order to fully follow Him to paradise, he would have to become poor, giving away all of his material wealth.

Losing wealth, security, and comfort is not a desirable thing. Become poor to become blessed? On the surface, it doesn't make sense. Even if the wealthy man did see the deeper reason, understanding the fulfillment of centering in God completely, he also knew that it would be a very difficult thing to do. It wasn't exactly what he was looking for or what he had wanted, and he walked away with a heavy heart. Loving this young man, Jesus did not call out after him and change His directive in order to make it easier on the poor guy. Nope. He let him walk away. We don't even know if that young man came back, if he was able to receive the gift that Jesus was offering him in deeply and radically loving the Lord. Was he willing to be poor physically but rich spiritually?

Are we?

When asking, in the name of Jesus, for something that we desire, we must be willing to trust in God's love and to trust God in knowing what is truly and eternally best for us and those we love. We must be willing to receive the answer to our prayers—even if the answer is undesired—remembering that truly asking for something in Jesus's name means being willing to receive *as Jesus Himself received*. Sometimes, it will be excruciating. God knows. We may suffer with Him, but through divine love, we will also rise with Him. In the big picture, all things will ultimately and eternally work together for *good* for those who love God.[44]

[44] See Romans 8:28.

4

See, I Am Doing Something New

*On the Radical Change That Christ Brings
and the Radical Change That Is Christ:
The Story of Zacchaeus, Vocations,
and Christ's Last Night,
Introduced by My Crooked Smile*

Joy: "Why Are You So Happy?"

"I just have to tell you—you have the most beautiful smile that I have ever seen," the usherette in the theater lobby told me, before a performance of Haydn's *The Creation*. I smiled all the more because it was far from the first time that someone had so complimented my smile, and I think it's rather funny. You see, I do not have a physically beautiful smile at all. It's a bit askew and shows a lot of upper gum, as well as an overbite and two overlapping teeth. The funny part is that, despite these marks of ugliness, there seems to be a whole lot of objective beauty in my smile, as so many different people have pointed it out. So . . . what makes it beautiful?

Joy makes it beautiful. The fact that I am crumpled up in a wheelchair, head flopped over, *and* genuinely smiling with an obvious joy takes some people's breath away—more so than if my smile actually were the most physically beautiful smile that they had ever seen.

People also often tell me that I am a happy person, saying it with surprise and wonder as they look at me, diseased and disabled. When I was younger, I was a bit taken aback and put off by their surprise. Sometimes, it made me want to fight against being called happy, wanting people to understand that I was just like them, capable of unhappiness, of frustration and sorrow. I wanted them to know that my smile isn't from obliviousness.

And I wondered why I *shouldn't* be happy. Yes, my life is extremely limited and difficult. However, being gifted by God with gratitude, I knew that there was great goodness in my life—a loving family, a safe home, comfort, and plenty—the natural causes for happiness. Coming into adulthood and trying to better understand life, the world, and other people, I would ask myself the question: Why is happiness such an unexpected thing to find in me that people consider it so remarkable?

Now that I am grown and better understand what true happiness means, I better appreciate the wonder with which so many people meet my easily and genuinely smiling self.

You see, we fallible human beings think that happiness comes through things, that it is attached to stuff like health, wealth, good looks, or fame. We think those things are what bring happiness, but there are plenty of people who are healthy, wealthy, good-looking, famous—and miserable. Although they may experience fleeting feelings of happiness, they don't know real, deep, *abiding* happiness (which I like to call *joy* to distinguish from the mere feeling, and because "happy" used to strike me as a sappy-sounding word). Many "well-off" people live unhappy lives of meaninglessness, addiction, anger, and loneliness because real happiness, *joy*, doesn't come as an attachment.

Real happiness has no strings attached. Joy is free. It comes freely, like a true gift.

We all thirst for joy as if we were specifically designed for it. That's because we are. We are, each and every one of us, created to be joyful. I believe that our Creator is loving, is Love itself, and joy is freely given to everyone through His love, like rain pouring down upon us. But we can only receive joy if our hearts, like bowls, are open, upturned, like a beggar's. Like beggars, we must know that we are dependent upon God who is the center and source of the truly and deeply good things of life. In that state, which is humble gratitude, our little bowls fill up and overflow, and we can drink our fill of joy. If, however, we are turned in upon ourselves, self-centered, upside down, then we are closed off from the reception of joy, and, though we may get wet, we will never be filled, never be satisfied.

Joy, then, which is what I believe people see in me, is not contingent upon a desirable body or prestige. That is why some-one like me—someone crumpled up in a wheelchair, severely dependent and limited in my abilities, choices, and lifestyle—can be joyful. I don't go out and look for joy (which is good because I don't get out much, and when I do it's not very far), and I also don't wait for joy to fall big and obvious into my lap. To some, the joy of living fully means experiencing as many *things* as possible, like trips to exotic locales, romantic hookups, physical thrills, luxuries, lauded accomplishments, and so forth. But again, this is the false concept that joy, that fullness of life, comes through things.

It doesn't. Real happiness is free and unconditional—neces-sarily so in order to be abiding joy. Otherwise it could be lost. When all things are gone—physical abilities, money, work, home, friends, small pleasures, even loved ones and mental abili-ties—*true joy remains*. This is because true joy is a oneness with life itself, with ultimate reality—with God. It is how I have come to think of righteousness. It's not about having the right answers, proper formulas, or desired things. Righteousness is holiness; it's being locked into the good, the true, and the beautiful. It's having a key of *love and gratitude* that fits into paradise.

Joy is Christ.

Joy is the wonder of letting God love you, through everything, and through the absence of things.

I am not perfect. I make mistakes, I miss the mark, I forget, ignore, hesitate, and wish away. Still, I believe that deep inside of me dwells, as in a sacred abode, infinite and eternal God. With this infinite source and eternal core, I have nothing to lose, and I am never abandoned. I am given the capacity to live infinitely and eternally with Love, with Truth, with Life itself.

With the Lord as our loving stronghold, of what shall we be afraid?[45]

This surrendering of fear is how we experience true joy, true peace. While I have fears and sorrows, angst and rage, disappointments and frustrations, just like all of us do because we are human, these are feelings that wash over on the surface, like clouds across the sky. Clouds can certainly change the weather and bring terrible storms, but they can never *remove* the sky. Knowing this truth is the beginning of joy, though not its fulfillment. For now, I see only dimly, know only in part.[46] My begging bowl is full and overflowing but will remain finite, limited, until I am taken up fully into the Infinite Source, eternally submerged in the eternal embrace of joy, which is God's pure and limitless love.

An Important Note

Sometimes, we might be less able to open up our little begging bowls because of mental illness, including depression or serious psychological trauma. Then we will need others to help us lift our hands and turn our little cups right-side up.

[45] See Psalms 27:1.
[46] See 1 Corinthians 13:12.

Also, for people like me, who have always been surrounded by loving human beings, it is certainly easier to recognize and be grateful for the goodness all around. Likewise, it is easier to become dependent on these loving human beings for happiness, which isn't real happiness at all. Such is my blessing and my challenge.

Because my family has been so good to me, I believe that it has been easier for me to be a happy person. However, I have also been a selfish person (as I still have a tendency to be), and, in my self-centeredness, my teens and twenties were ridden with as much bone-shaking sorrow as hormones and loneliness can ravage on a young person—especially a young person so continually denied by circumstance. Thankfully, I was created with a loving family, a healthy sense of humor, and the ability to find beauty in the ordinary. These gifts and attributes allowed me my first experiences of happiness. I thought that, because of these experiences, I knew what real happiness was. But I only discovered *true joy* when I began to learn about *true love*—love that is not contingent upon pleasure, affection, security, or even familial ties.

Familial love, though sacredly beautiful and good, too often can become centered on the self, on "what's in it for me," because that bond provides things such as security. True love (which is found in authentic familial, filial, and marital bonds) is not loving for my own sake, but for the sake of the other—at the cost of sacrificing myself. This is self-giving love, agape, divine love. My parents had always given me this example of genuine love, but although I knew that they loved me, I didn't see or comprehend the deep core of divine love that they were reflecting.

I learned of it only in coming to know Christ on the Cross.

Infinite and eternal, the all-powerful God humbled Himself to become a human being and gives Himself wholly and completely to us in love. He thirsts for us and rains His love down upon us. Whether we receive Him or not, whether we receive His love or not, He gives Himself anyway, totally and unconditionally. His love, God Himself, is our joy. In knowing this kind of love — true love, divine love — I grew in my understanding and experiencing of true joy.

Allowing God to open me up to divine love is why I am a joyful person and why there is great beauty in my gummy little smile.

Closer to God: The Story of Zacchaeus

God loves me. God loves you. God loves, well ... everybody. None of us earn God's love; none of us can do anything to merit its eternal outpouring. God's love is a perfectly pure and free gift, given to us before He even formed us in the womb.[47] Yet, we sometimes think that there are some people who God may love a little more than others. This, however, is impossible. God loves each and every one of us *infinitely*, and not even God can love more than infinitely.

If we think that we know someone who is especially loved by God, what we are really witnessing is that particular person's *response* to God—and all of the wonders that God can accomplish through any human being who is open to the prompting of the Holy Spirit and is willing to be divinely loved.

A person who is poor or disabled, for example, may seem closer to God because she bears her suffering patiently and is a joyful, loving person. However, the poverty or disability itself does not make the person inherently closer to God, to God's peace and beauty. In fact, suffering and limitations can often cause a person to close in upon herself, tempting her toward self-centeredness,

---

[47] See Jeremiah 1:5.

self-pity, and away from God's love. Rather, when a person is strong through adversity and joyful even in hardships, it means that she has chosen to respond to God's universal call to holiness and willingly allowed her heart to be opened to embrace the presence of God, to receive and give divine love in her life.

Let us reflect upon this concept as we look at the biblical story of Zacchaeus.

Zacchaeus was a short man, remarkably short, and St. Luke says that, because of his shortcoming, "he could not see"[48] in a crowd. He was unable. Although we wouldn't call him disabled, he definitely had a physical disadvantage because of his height. This handicap, if you will, did not make him a good person. He was a tax collector: nothing specifically wrong with that, but he was a wealthy one. And a wealthy tax collector in the day of Jesus was one who took more than what was required of him to take. He profited by demanding extra money from his neighbors, using the might of the Roman Empire to get it.

Despite being the noted sinner that he was, lacking a close relationship with God, he was curious about Jesus. Who wouldn't be curious about a charismatic healer in town? Although other unscrupulous people could have satisfied their curiosity by just standing on the side of the road and casually watching Jesus go by, Zacchaeus could not. His limitation meant that he couldn't be casual. Another severely short person in the same situation may have simply decided that satisfying his curiosity about Jesus wasn't worth the extra physical effort required to see. But not Zacchaeus. Zacchaeus made the extra effort necessary to achieve his goal: he climbed up a Sycamore tree in order to get a closer look.

[48] Luke 19:3.

It was this willingness to go the extra mile that caught the attention of Jesus, who was planning on simply passing through the town.

Jesus knew that Zacchaeus was a physically encumbered man and an unscrupulous one. But when the Holy Spirit prompted Zacchaeus to meet Jesus (as it will prompt every human being to seek and find Christ), Zacchaeus not only didn't refuse the prompting, he went out of his way to answer it—a blessed response to God's presence. By climbing that tree, Zacchaeus opened up his heart to enter into a true relationship with Christ. Jesus said to him, "Zacchaeus, come down quickly, for today I must stay at your house."[49]

With those words from God Incarnate, Zacchaeus swiftly descended from the tree. He brought himself down low, repentant, joyful to receive Christ, and ready and willing to make amends for all of the wrong that he had done in his life. Again, he was willing to go the extra mile, giving half of his possessions to the poor and repaying those whom he had extorted four times over. He chose to change his life radically for the glory of God.

In a way, Zacchaeus's physical disadvantage was a kind of gift in that he could not respond merely casually to his craving to seek the Divine. His adversity gave him the opportunity to thoughtfully choose: either go about his business ignoring the inner call or commit himself to the quest and the hard work needed to fulfill it. His choice to commit and focus enabled him, despite his previously sinful disposition, to be open to receive God's transformative love.

Whenever any of us, able-bodied or not, imitate Zacchaeus, willing to give more of ourselves to answer the Spirit, to bare

[49] Luke 19:5.

our vulnerabilities, to put ourselves out on a limb to meet the Lord, we find ourselves close to God and better able to receive Christ with joy.

May we all, in sickness and in health, in good times and in bad, heed the call of the Holy Spirit and be willing to put in the extra effort, expose our souls, and go above and beyond to seek and find Christ.

Casting into the Deep

I have longed for a normal life. (Sometimes.)

Of course, I want the normal, simple things, like walking and feeding myself, but these most basic desires aren't the ones that have most often overwhelmed me with pining, mourning, and grieving. It's the very common human desires for marriage, children, and a home of my own that have filled my dreams and imagination and racked my body with sorrowful aching.

These unrealized dreams for a normal life are not exclusive to people like me — the severely physically disabled or mentally impaired. Most humans have common desires for the "ideal life." Although it is more idyllic in dreams than in reality, other people's failures do not stop our longings. I've often tried to comfort myself for my lack of a husband and kids with the thought that marriage and motherhood aren't all that they're cracked up to be. Even a normal life is difficult and trying, with its own serious heartbreaks. I know. Still ... I think I would take one — headaches, sorrows, failures, and all — if I could.

But I can't.

This is my life. My way of daily living is how many, many people live all around the world, dependent upon others and limited in their social interactions and achievements — and there is absolutely nothing *inhuman* about it. I'm not afraid, however, to say that it is abnormal. I can easily call it abnormal without feeling any shame or inferiority because I know that there is nothing wrong with being *different*. Christ was different. The Word was made flesh to cause us to live *differently*—even radically.

The childhood of God Incarnate was pretty normal. So normal was Christ's upbringing, in fact, that His neighbors, who had watched Him grow up, were appalled at Him for claiming to be anything other than ordinary and ran Him out of His own hometown.[50] Jesus deliberately departed from His normal life, moving out of His widowed mother's house and giving up the carpentry trade that He had learned from His foster father to set out on an itinerant teaching ministry. Yet even this wandering Rabbi kind of life was not completely uncommon in Jesus's time, and the disciples, or students, that He gathered around Him were normal people taken from ordinary life. He chose fishermen, a common trade on the Sea of Galilee, and even a tax collector. These were normal guys doing normal things—until Jesus came along.

That's when life became different.

As St. Luke tells it in his Gospel, Jesus, at the beginning of His ministry, used the boat of Simon and his brother Andrew as a kind of pulpit to preach to the crowds that wanted to hear from Him. When He was done speaking to them, He told Simon to put the boat out into deep water and cast his net. Simon didn't really want to do this; he didn't see the sense in it since they had been working hard all night and hadn't caught anything. Nevertheless, he decided to put his trust in Jesus and did, indeed, cast into the depths. The result was an enormous haul of fish

[50] See Matthew 13:54–58, Luke 4:16–30.

that nearly caused the boat to sink. Simon had a glimpse, then, of the supernatural, of who Jesus really was.

Fear of the Lord is the tremulous awe of knowing that God is God—and we are not. From this wondrous humility, this catch of the breath that surrenders absolutely to absolute majesty—from this, all wisdom derives. After Simon pulled in the miraculous catch, he fell down before Jesus in awe, declaring himself unworthy to be in the presence of the Lord.

But Jesus pulled him deeper into the divine presence, in order to radically change Simon's life, as well as to change Simon himself. "Do not be afraid," Jesus said, "from now on you will be catching men."[51] Simon heard the word of God and believed. He leapt up in faith and, trusting in Christ, humbly and boldly, left the normal things of his own life to follow God's call. This simple fisherman who had collapsed in fear of the Lord would be transformed, even renamed "the rock," upon which Christ would build His Church.

That's what a true encounter with Christ does—revolutionizes us.

God did not become one of us in order to maintain the status quo among human beings. He came to be radically different. This doesn't mean that every person who lives a life other than the norm is Christlike, nor does it mean that a person cannot be Christlike in an ordinary life. Christ blessed the normalcy of marriage by performing a miracle at a wedding celebration, and He upheld the values of simple, normal life in His historical time through the parables of everyday living that He told. Meanwhile, He called every person, whether living a normal life or not, to live a *radical* life of love.

[51] Luke 5:10.

Christ deepened the divine commandment, "Do not kill," by teaching that we should not have anger in our hearts against our brothers and utter insults against them.[52] "Love your enemies,"[53] Jesus tells us, exhorting us to forgive more than seven times our brothers and sisters who sin against us — more like seventy-seven times.[54] When a person strikes us across the face, we are called to offer the assailant the other cheek to strike as well.[55] "Whoever wishes to come after me," Christ said, "must deny himself, take up his cross, and follow me."[56] Jesus beckoned His listeners to a new order, to a different way of looking at things.

Though revolutionary, Christ Jesus was not a rebel without a cause. Yes, He was boldly defiant of the established order, but only when the establishment went against the divine order of merciful love. Jesus bucked against the pride and greed that had taken a stranglehold on the living of human life and called people out of complacency into deeper examination of their lives and hearts — into a deeper relationship with their Creator.

The vast majority of people in Jesus's time, however, dismissed Him or just flat out never encountered Him. Most people continued to complacently live their ordinary lives without any profound wonder, without any ego-shattering gratitude, without any radical departure from self-centeredness, without any deep sacrifices for love.

That still happens today among those of us who call ourselves Christians. How many of us allow the Word of God to slice

[52] See Matthew 5:21–24.
[53] Matthew 5:44.
[54] See Matthew 18:22.
[55] See Matthew 5:39.
[56] Matthew 16:24.

through us like a sword? How many of us are willing to disappoint our parents or siblings or even children in the name of truth and holiness?[57] How many of us are truly willing to "put out into deep water," to cast into the depths? God often asks us to do radical things — but nothing that He wasn't willing to do Himself when He lived His human life upon this Earth.

So, I ask myself: *What am I willing to do?*

Yes, I would have liked to have been married. I would've liked that to have been my calling, but not because that life would have been any easier than the one that I am living now. A Christian marriage is exclusive and demanding. It's a daily, lifelong challenge because God is asking every person who is living the normal life of spouse, children, and home to love radically. To dig deep. To *sacrifice*. To give without expecting a return. To care selflessly for family and for neighbor. Why? Because in this deeper way of living, this calling to a life beyond the mere surface of things, abides divine truth, love, and joy everlasting — the wondrously profound reality of human fulfillment.

God invites every human being to be revolutionized. Some of us are called to love radically in the commonly desired modes of life, as in marriage and parenthood. Some of us are called to love radically in uncommonly desired modes, as in the priesthood, the consecrated religious life, or single professionalism. And some of us are called to love radically in modes of life that are not desired at all, as in dependency brought about through serious ailment of some kind. What is *normal* about all of these different ways of living is their capacity for *revolutionary love*. What is *common* in these diverse and complementary modes of Christianity is *holiness*, a word that can be translated to mean "other than."

---

[57] See Matthew 10:34–35.

We are made to be other than shallow. We are called to break through the surface of things to the inner depths of our hearts, of life, of every human being. Jesus tells us to "put out into deep water."[58] This command often seems to go against what is viewed as sensible and rational, but if we, like the disciples Simon and Andrew, can overcome our skepticism and trust Jesus, then we will be amazed at the abundance of treasure found in the depths.

Christians are called to be countercultural. This is certainly true in our current mainstream culture, but, in fact, it has always been true of Christianity. Even when the Christian Faith was the state-sponsored and promulgated religion of the Roman Empire, Christians had to resist the cultural temptations toward materialism and self-righteousness in order to truly live the Faith. These are the temptations that we still need to resist today. The temptations that *I* need to resist today ... and today ... and today....

Each and every human being is made to be unique and to live a *peculiarly Christian life*. I am not like you, and you are not like me, and yet we have an essential and eternal commonality that we cannot escape without running away from truth itself. We are, each and every one of us, loved into being by God and given particular gifts and vocations to reflect His self-giving love in the world—*His radical love*. If we are content merely to rest on the surface of the world and do not radically cast into the deep, then we will not have a true and full encounter with Christ—we will not behold God and come to know God as He knows us. We will not be fulfilled.

I, like you, am being called by Christ to boldly break through the surface of my life and be pulled, be submerged, into the

---

[58] Luke 5:4.

depths of my own sanctity. I am called to humbly meet God there, face-to-face, heart-to-heart, and allow Him to embrace me completely in His transformative love. I am not called to exist in mere shallowness. I am meant to put out into deep waters.

There were periods in my life when I thought that I was relegated to the shore because my inabilities do not let me participate fully in the normal living of normal life, but I began to understand that some people who are living the normal life are either sitting on the shoreline or going out in little boats without ever casting into the deep. Neither disabilities nor abnormal modes of living exclude a person from casting out broadly and plunging into the depths. Self-centeredness, lust, sloth, pride, and greed—these are the things that prevent us from penetrating the surface of life and being immersed in the glory of God.

This little life of mine may not be the life that I would've chosen for myself, but I don't know what kind of life best beats with my heart and best corresponds to my eternal destiny. God, who made me, does. A deep treasure exists in my life, as in your life, no matter how normal or abnormal it may be. Will you be daring enough to dig deep and find it? Will I? Will we heed the call of God and be not afraid to love radically, to forgive freely, to sacrifice generously, and to recognize God's Word made flesh in every human being, including ourselves?

Will we trust in the Lord and, in tremulous awe and humility, fall at His feet, ready to be transformed?

And He Loved Them to the End

If you knew you were going to die, what would you do on your last day?

By choosing to become one of us, God chose to taste death. It is, perhaps, not precisely accurate to say that God died, because God is spirit, eternal, and, therefore, cannot die. But Jesus most certainly *did* die, and Jesus is God Incarnate, both God and man. By becoming fully human, Jesus would have to die bodily, fully experiencing what all humans experience through death. This very human man, Jesus, with His characteristics, tastes, and appetites, lived life with His family and friends, people whom He loved. There were people whose company He particularly enjoyed, as well as foods, times of day, songs, and activities in which He especially delighted.

And then came the day when He knew that it was all going to end.

Being fully divine, as well as fully human, Jesus knew when He was going to die. And He knew that He was going to be killed in a cruel and horrific way.

On the evening before His death, He gathered with His friends and shared a meal with them — His last meal. When He broke the bread and passed the cup of wine, He told them that it was His Body and Blood given up and poured forth for salvation, and that they were to eat and drink of His Body and Blood in continuing remembrance, or re-presentation, so that they could abide in Him and He in them.

His friends were perplexed.

After supper, He, the Lord, whom they called Master, bent low and washed their feet. They didn't really know why, although He tried to explain that He was leaving them an example of service in humble self-giving—an act of true love.

God Almighty was doing something radical in a very simple way. He was doing something truly new in the history of the world. And it all began when a young peasant woman named Mary was visited by an angel and willingly gave herself over to God's will, receiving His Word made flesh. It's beyond human thinking that such a simple person, such a little person, could be responsible for helping to set in motion God's revolutionary, humankind-saving plan. One might expect a noble queen, much admired and praised by all nations to be chosen for such a mission. Or a brave activist for justice and peace, noted far and wide for her wise and tireless work on behalf of others. Two thousand years ago, when few women held lofty positions, no one would have expected a girl who was barely a woman, hailing from the sticks, poor and unknown, to be chosen by God for this singular, cosmically significant role.

But God's ways are above man's ways. God had created Mary with special care and knew that she was the noblest, wisest, and bravest of people, whose selfless and tireless work as His mother would serve true justice and true peace for all nations.

It just wasn't apparent to anyone else.

Jesus Himself did not fit the expected part of the Messiah. Many thought, like the Apostle Nathaniel did on first hearing about Jesus, that nothing good could come out of Nazareth.[59] This man, Jesus, had been known in His hometown simply as the son of a carpenter, comparable to a modern-day construction worker, a trade that He Himself worked.

Furthermore, during His public ministry, He associated with society's undesirable types—not just the poor but also people who were considered immoral, like Roman tax collectors and prostitutes. None of this kept with the popular notion of who the Messiah would be. Surely, God's Chosen One would be a mighty ruler who would demand tribute, punish the wayward, and bring political stability and power to Israel. Or he would be a fierce warrior who would lead an army to war against Israel's enemies and violently throw them out once and for all.

No one envisioned that the violence to be done would be against the Messiah Himself. No one imagined that the power of the Savior would be manifested in weakness. No one truly understood that the freedom that God was bringing to His people was the freedom of humble obedience. No one comprehended that the restoration, which the Messiah would enact, was not of land possession, but rather the restoration of humankind to true images of God. Even the image of God was misunderstood. To truly reflect divinity, human beings are called not to dominance but to self-giving, self-emptying, sacrificial love for God and neighbor.

The true Messiah was the perfection of that love in human nature.

On the night before His death, Jesus, knowing what was coming, did not use His divine power to stop those who were going to kill Him, nor even to throw Himself a real humdinger of a farewell

---

[59] See John 1:46.

party. Rather, Jesus, God Incarnate, chose to be of service. He, who brought into existence every living thing, who has power over the life and death of every flesh and blood creature, gave His own Body and Blood *to be consumed* for our eternal sustenance. He, who is the Creator and Master of the entire universe, true God and true Lord, knelt down before mere men and tenderly washed their dirty feet.

That evening, Jesus tried to tell His friends the significance of everything that He was doing and of everything that was about to happen. He prayed aloud to His Father for their benefit, shared His hopes with them, gave them words of advice and encouragement, all the while knowing that they didn't get it and that it would take some time before they did. They boldly proclaimed that they would never abandon Him. But He knew that they would. One of them would even betray Him with a sign of affection, a kiss.

Jesus knew that He would have to go through the ordeal and horror of arrest, torture, and crucifixion without His beloveds' understanding or support. He even expressed frustration and a little exasperation when, as the evening drew on, His best friends fell asleep, though He had asked them to stay awake with Him in His sorrow. He said to Peter, "So you could not keep watch with me for one hour?"[60]

His companions could not grasp the profoundly awesome and beautiful gift that Jesus was giving them. They could not bear to see Him degraded, brought low, and put to death. Jesus wasn't angry with them, for He knew that this would happen. He was deeply saddened, however, scared and dreading what He needed to do. But He was willing to go through it anyway for

[60] Matthew 26:40.

their sake — even for the sake of the one who would hand Him over to those who despised Him, even for those very people who would seize, torture, and kill Him. Despite it being difficult for His loved ones to grasp, Jesus knew that the immensity of His pain and suffering was for their good, for the good of every human being on His beloved Earth. Being the divine Son of God, He knew and understood the mysterious way of God's salvation that was laid out before Him. Yet, being fully human, He was also sorrowful and terribly frightened about going through it.

Jesus, the divine Messiah, agonized the night before He died. He, left alone by His friends, sweat droplets of blood as He prayed. But He did not run away.

5

No Greater Love

On the Pains of Love:
The Value of Life, the Unity of the Cross,
and the Depths of Christ's Love,
Introduced by Christ in My Agony

The Way of the Cross

Sometimes, life is unbearable.

In the midst of illness, everyday tasks of survival can be an overwhelming struggle. In the midst of pain, both thought and breath have cutting edges of sharp immediacy. The suffering of human life is a difficult burden, sometimes seemingly impossible to carry—the body weak and exhausted, the mind desperate and despairing. Sometimes life seems pointless or cruel. Suffering can make life awful and even undesirable.

God knows.

The heavy instrument of His death, which was strapped to His back, crashed down on Him with each fall, crushing His chest to knock the air out of His lungs. Smashed flat on His face, hard on the rocky pavement, the thorns that encircled His head stabbed into the tender flesh of His ear and eyelid. Jesus gasped and cried out in agony. The beam across His shoulders pressed mercilessly into His flailed skin, the deep gouges and bloody tears of flesh piercing, burning, ripping anew with exquisite and mind-exploding pain. How could He go on? After hours and hours of torture, shackled, dragged, beaten, scourged, beaten and tortured some more, He was now forced to march to His death. Why? Why are human beings so cruel? And why is the human body capable of being so terribly and horribly inflamed with pain?

I fall on my face with Jesus, kicked repeatedly upon the ground by my affliction, each blow finding new places of torment, each moment seized with anguish. The miseries of a day, mind or body wracked with suffering, find me carrying the burden of the Cross with Christ, who fell again and again beneath the weight of love.

Only love could inspire the All-Powerful to become so weak and pitiful beside me, wincing with every biting torture that He and I experience, sweating and sobbing with me for relief to come, doubled over and horrified again when the suffering only gets worse.

How did He go on? *Why* did He go on? When the sufferer is God Incarnate, why does He not stop His suffering? With a wave of His hand, why does He not choose to bring the whole horrific misery to an end?

Why? *Because I can't.*

I can't stop my own pain. So Christ, loving me inexorably, chose not to stop His, so that He is with me always.

I am limited. I live my life in an imperfect place, a world fallen from grace beneath the lures of pride and greed, where nobody can see clearly, so we grope and shove and fall even further down.

Down in the murky sludge, I might forget the place from which I have come, the pure flower that bore me forth as a living soul, fragrant and light and made for a celestial home. I may forget that this soul of mine exists within the divine creation of my body and that my body, like my life, is a rich and sumptuous gift. I may forget that my soul and my body unite in one unique person, *me*, so that the fruit that is my particular humanity may hang with heavy beauty upon the tree of life, ripe with love and possibility. Though I slip and crash upon the ground, tread underfoot, holes rotting through my flesh, the seeds of my eternity will taste no corruption. Christ, the Word of God made flesh, holds them in His Sacred Heart, which, though it beats with the agony of this fallen place, though it is pierced through and torn open by the fallen, never forgets, never loses sight, never succumbs to the despair that is felt when lying crushed upon the bloody ground.

He will rise up. *I* will rise up. We will rise up together.

Though we collapse again and again, we will rise. We will rise and rise until our nature becomes the act of rising—painful, exhausting, overwhelming, but *rising*. And then, when rising is perfected within us, we will soar.

Jesus ascended into glory far above and beyond this fallen world, but He does not leave me behind. He lovingly carries me within the wounds given to Him in this place, the wounds upon His body where my own wounded body finds compassion, rest, and the way home.

The hardness of this place, this human life, breaks the glistening red and gold of the fruit that we are, miraculously yielding the sacred sweetness within us. Some won't allow it. Some will merely break and crumble, wasting away, lost in the torments of the place. But some will rise.

I will lift my eyes above the murkiness to see the face of my God streaked with blood, with tears, with mud, and *with love*. I will bare my soul to Him and allow Him to love me. With His strength, I will rise and look around at the beautiful faces, the loving hands reaching out. I will see the terrible beauty of a world often ignorant of its own sacred radiance, an unknowing world shining bright and resplendent with other living souls rising within. The gift of this place ... the gift of this place is breathtaking. This place, this life is how we come to know love—bodily, gritty, biting, catching, piercing love. It will knock the breath out of you, it will bring you to your knees, it will spear right through you. And it will raise you up.

Here is the exquisite bliss and sublime majesty of *love*.

Stripped

What are you worth?

Perhaps you're thinking about how much money you may have in your bank account or the value of the property you may own; the possible benefits from your life insurance policy or what you get paid for doing your job. Or perhaps you are thinking of the work that you do for your family, your friends, or your community, and you're calculating that productivity into cost.

But what if you were stripped of all of your possessions—and even stripped of your physical abilities? What would you be worth, then?

Jesus knew the poverty of the manger and of the Cross. He knew the fragility and abject dependency of the womb and of infancy, His helpless body laid in the borrowed feeding trough of animals. He knew the deprivation of being a prisoner and a murder victim, His very clothes stripped off of Him by Roman soldiers who gambled for possession of them, and His arms and legs nailed fast so that He couldn't even hold on to life.

What was Jesus worth?

Jesus owned no property and had no bank account or paycheck. He was a poor man. In the end, He didn't even own the clothes on His back. He had nothing. And yet ...

Was there a richer man who ever lived?

The entire universe is His, and His is the earth with its abundant variety of fruits and grains, silver and diamonds, gold and timber, oil and pearls, and living creatures of sultry fur, shimmering scales, and vibrant plumage. Perhaps, now, you are mentally putting a price on all of these things to say, "Yes, Jesus, as the Son of God, was an extremely wealthy man." But you're blind if that's how you see His worth. You have brain-damage from sin if you calculate His value in *things*.

The earth does not belong to Jesus in the sense of human ownership, but rather in the sense of divine creation, generation, and source. The universe is His masterwork; all laws that shape and govern it were written and established by Him who is God. But God doesn't *have* the universe. God doesn't *possess* the earth. As His beloved Creation, the earth eternally *belongs* to the loving heart of God, but God is not possessive in the sense of greed. God lovingly gave His Creation away.

He gave the earth and all within it to *us*, His beloved ones, for our good. God owns nothing. God is *materially* poor.

And so, God-made-man is materially poor. At the end of His earthly life, Jesus owned nothing, letting Himself be stripped of the few things that He possessed as a human being. Yet He was *rich* because He was fully in communion with His Father's divine love. He was wealthy, not in terms of possession, of what He could own and use, but in terms of loving—of all that He could give away.

Jesus holds on to nothing as He is stripped and nailed to the Cross. His hands are empty as He reaches out to us with only His love. In pain, while dying, *weak* and *poor*, He *powerfully* and *generously* bestows the greatest wealth: mind-blowing forgiveness to the soldiers who stripped Him, ego-shattering redemption to those who mocked Him, and earthshaking love to all who would see Him dead. Only in the most demeaned and lowest condition, in the poorest and least powerful state of life, could God Incarnate give these treasures beyond compare, these treasures that only infinite and eternal God can give.

Think about it. If Christ had been enthroned in earthly glory as a rightful king, then we would have seen merely the richness of His scepter and crown and the power of His commands instead of the incalculable force of His self-giving love. If He had lived as a monetarily wealthy man, distributing wealth to the tangibly poor in order to grant them financial security, then we would have remained blind and deaf to *true joy*, with the damage from our sins left unhealed, so that we would have continued to place our worth in mere things and our levels of productivity.

Jesus reveals to us that we are worth infinitely more than that.

The man who was crucified beside Jesus, whom you may know as the penitent thief, was also stripped. Not only was he stripped of his possessions and his mobility in being nailed to a cross (before being stripped of his earthly life), he also had his heart and soul stripped bare by the grace of humility and repentance. He knew that he was guilty of committing the crime for which he was receiving the prescriptive punishment and, so, accepted his death on the cross. By letting himself be so naked and vulnerable before God, only love remained in him, and he was able to recognize the true identity of Jesus.

The condemned man on the other side, however, reviled Jesus, telling Him that if He was truly the Messiah, then He should take them all off of their crosses and spare them from this death. The penitent thief rebuked him, saying, "Have you no fear of God?"[61] The penitent one knew that they were sharing

---

[61] Luke 23:40.

the same ignominious and torturous death with, not only an innocent man who didn't deserve it, but *the King of Eternity*. He was in awe beside his King.

The Lord of All chose to suffer beside criminals, to die with them. *O wondrous love*.

Jesus and the penitent thief both knew the worth of the other.

Filled with wonder, the humble and repentant criminal was able, because of his stripped heart, to see Jesus as True King and, sensing a shadow of his own profound worth as a human being, spoke to the Holy One, asking for remembrance in His Kingdom. To him, Jesus said, "Amen, I say to you, today you will be with me in paradise."[62]

Christ lived among us and died for us to reveal the truth about ourselves. The unfathomable depths of who we are, and of what our true value is, can only be glimpsed when we are pure in heart and poor in spirit—when we allow ourselves to be stripped of worldliness and self-centeredness and become humble beggars before God. Then, and only then, will our eyes be opened to see.

So, what *are* you worth?

You are worth God becoming a poor, tortured man so that He may show you His Divine Face and pour into your heart the endless treasure of His Divine Love. You are worth eternal love and the ceaseless generosity of Heaven. If you need proof of your infinite worth, then gaze upon the crucifix and think how low the Son of God is willing to make Himself in order for you to be able to know Him and receive Him into your own stripped heart. Ponder, with humble acceptance and loving gratitude, all that He selflessly gives away so that *you* may be sublimely rich in eternal glory.

[62] Luke 23:43.

INRI

What do you think of when you see a crucifix?

A young cousin of mine once asked me what the letters at the top of the crucifix, INRI, signify. I could have simply given her the answer, that those letters are an abbreviation for what Pontius Pilate had written on Jesus's Cross: *Iesus Nazarenus Rex Iudaeorum*, which is Latin for, "Jesus the Nazarene, King of the Jews."[63] I could have told her that right off, but I didn't. Instead, I first replied with a joke: INRI stands for, "I'm Nailed Right In." Ba-dum bum.

When a friend of mine had originally told me the joke, a quip that she had heard a pastor tell his congregation, I had giggled, but I also winced a little, feeling as though I was making light of a loved one's pain. My motive for retelling the joke may have been well intended, to show that Catholics don't need to be dour and gravely serious all the time, that we have a sense of humor, but I admit that I was also spurred by my desire to prove that I'm just like everybody else—flippant about the sacred. I regretted my choice, fearing what irreverent repercussions it might have for my little cousin. Would that joke now be stuck in her head whenever she looked upon a crucifix?

[63] John 19:19.

For me, the crucifix is no joke. It's an exquisitely profound symbol of God's love, God's humility, God's selflessness. The crucifix, like the crucifixion itself, is the truth of abiding love — and the excruciating pain that love is willing to endure — held up as a sign of victory over death and destruction. *Oh, Mystery of Mysteries.*

Christ on the Cross answers the most common faith question: "If God is loving, then why does God allow suffering?"

Answer:

"Look to the crucifix."

We suffer. God knows. But He doesn't let us to do anything that He isn't willing to do *with* us, that He isn't willing to suffer *Himself.*

How could I make light of that? Before I became too hard on myself for what I felt was a terrible mistake, however, I thought about why a Christian pastor may have included that quip in his sermon.

I'm Nailed Right In

How many times in your life have you been held back or frustrated by your own limitations? Have you ever wanted something with your whole heart, something good and beautiful, and been unable to reach it? Have you loved something, or someone, and watched it slip away from you? Have you ever found yourself in an undesirable situation and felt miserably trapped?

These are the times when *you* are nailed right in.

I'm nailed right in.

So was God Incarnate.

Jesus was beaten, tortured, and stripped. Iron spikes were pounded through His flesh, securing His hands and feet with horrifically searing pain to wooden beams. He was trapped by the fear, greed, and power lust of others. He was imprisoned upon a cross, with no mercy, no escape.

God *knows* what it feels like to be weak, to be fragile, to be at the mercy of others who have no mercy. God knows what it feels like to be unable, to be *disabled*, to be physically helpless. God *chose* to let Himself know this. And whenever we are likewise weak, fragile, or helpless, as well as all of the small moments when we feel trapped, when we feel stuck, we need only to look to the crucifix to know love ... *real love* ... and to know that we are not alone. In the sight of Christ on the Cross, we can understand that God has infinite and intimate compassion for us, that God really knows how it feels to suffer, for He is suffering with us. In seeing the extent of God's love, in seeing how far God is willing to go to prove His love for us and to raise us up from our fallen world, we can sense something of the awesome power found in following Him.

As St. Paul said about his own suffering, "I will rather boast most gladly of my weaknesses, in order that the power of Christ may dwell with me."[64] The unlimited force of love comes through our human limitations when we let God transform us into instruments of His love.

There is divine strength in all of our "cannots": the strength of acceptance that braves every fear and sorrow, every pain and weakness, as we humbly trust, in faith and hope, that God will make something eternally beautiful out of them. Trusting in God, we can realize this courageous strength in our lives and participate in eternal beauty by loving God, ourselves, and others as Christ loves from the Cross—intimately and infinitely. To receive the

[64] 2 Corinthians 12:9.

outpouring of God's love upon the Cross is to know that God's compassionate love conquers all.

God is truly with us. We are *nailed right in*, pinioned, held fast with Christ, who chooses to suffer with us out of love for us. We are pinioned by grace and held fast by divine love to the heart of God. Though bound by the sufferings of this fallen world, we are, through them, embraced by the boundlessness of God's love, because God binds Himself so utterly and painstakingly to us. He is *nailed right into* our lives.

See? His arms are opened wide, His heart is bursting open—for love of *you*.

My Soul to the Netherworld

Have you ever submerged yourself under water, such as in a lake or a pool, and gone down, down, down? The light, if visible, is far off and distorted, while all around you, enshrouding you, is a seductive, dulling kind of darkness. There's an oblivious kind of quiet down there that feels rather pleasing, and you would stay below.

But within you is the instinct to rise.

You are made to rise—from the pool, from the self-pity, the grudge, the addiction. You are created to rise up, to see clearly, to breathe deeply, to break free.

You are made for the Light.

However ... what if your ability to rise is deadened by self-abuse—by the damages of sin? Then, all that is good within you would drown. It is for this reason that Jesus gave Himself in sacrifice on the Cross: to save you wherever you are. He descended to the dead so that He may always be with you, so that He may be intimately with you even in the deepest, darkest abyss. No matter how far down you go, Christ is there with you. Christ Jesus is there; He stretches out His hand and parts the drowning waters. You need only to reach out for His mercy and He will take hold of you, and He will raise you up to the land of the living, to the Light.

6

A Place for You

On the Reality of Our Eternal Destinies:
Christ's Resurrection, the Ascension,
and the Assumption of the Virgin Mary,
Introduced by My Wariness of Hope

The Hope of Heaven

Having been given a life expectancy of thirteen years, I have been wondering about death and facing the knowledge of my own impending demise since I was a child. Although I have lived my predicted lifespan three times over (and still going, thanks be to God), I know for certain that I will not live to see old age. My survival is very fragile. A simple chest cold can kill me. I don't know for exactly how long my earthly life will continue, but I treat each year as though it may be my last — and that is a more deeply appreciative, joyful, and wondrous experience than you might think. The acknowledgment of early death hasn't made me gloomy, depressed, or pessimistic. For me, it has simply meant that I'm not afraid to think, ask, or talk about the *fullness* of life, which includes death.

It doesn't mean, however, that I'm not afraid of dying.

Who isn't at least slightly terrified at the possibility of prolonged suffering, weakening, and pain in the act of dying? Even Jesus was filled with agonizing dread the night before He died, knowing that His passing over was going to be horribly torturous and literally excruciating. And then there is, added to my fear of the dying process, my fearful loathing of leaving — of leaving this terribly beautiful life and all of my dearly loved ones. This is not something that I want to do. I don't want to say goodbye. And yet, I know that I must. There will come a time for each and every one of us when we must leave this sacred blue and green home that we have loved so very much.

You might reasonably think that the hope of Heaven — the hope of the soul never dying and an eternal life of pure bliss — has helped to alleviate my fear and bring me comfort. But ... well ... I am too often wary of hope, even, I confess, the hope that is a theological virtue: the desire and expectation of Heaven. Perhaps this comes from childhood hopes unfulfilled.

For two years, I was a poster child for my disease, asking for donations on the local TV cutaways of the MDA Labor Day Telethon and attending fundraisers throughout my state. The goal of all of this was to garner donations to fund research that would bring about a cure for my disease — this was, indeed, the great hyped-up hope. "Hope for a Cure" was a continuous slogan and, within the Muscular Dystrophy Association of the 1980s, parents and patients alike seemed to really believe that it would happen any day. But it didn't. My mother tells me that I wanted to be able to walk before I started school and that I believed becoming a poster child would make that happen. But it didn't.

These hopes of mine were obviously not fulfilled. I don't remember being hurt by the disappointment, probably because I don't remember the hope itself. Knowing me, I no doubt felt rather foolish having hoped for something that didn't come. Later, with teenaged amusement, I would sarcastically point out that hope is a four-letter word.

So when it comes to Heaven, well ... it's still as if I don't want to believe in anything that might be too good to be true. Subconsciously, I might not want to be hurt by disappointment again. And quite consciously, I don't want to be a fool, believing in something that isn't real. There are many intelligent people, after all, who believe that Heaven is impossible and that any hope for it is mere wishful thinking.

The fact, however, is that it would be foolish arrogance to think that something exists only if we, limited creatures, can physically detect it or scientifically prove it. Do we really think that full knowledge of all that is within and beyond the cosmos can fit into our finite brains? God certainly cannot, and the created world that we experience with our bodily senses is not everything that God has created. As images of God, we have spiritual souls that we cannot perceive with our senses of sight, hearing, touch, smell, or taste. And there is another "world" that we are similarly unable to physically detect — what we call the heavenly realm.

Resurrected in glorified body, Jesus ascended into Heaven, which we are unable to perceive while still in our earthly states of being. There, we will also go in union with Christ — if we truly follow Him in our earthly lives. Then, our heavenly destinies will be joined with His for all eternity. This is what we are told by Jesus, what we are promised. And we believe. We live and act by faith. If Heaven is as we Christians believe — the pure and eternal embrace of God, endless love, glory, and bliss — then what fool would not desire it?

So what if the world looks at me as though I'm foolish for having such a hope? Isn't it an ultimately noble and glorious thing to be a fool for Christ?[65] If I am a faithful believer, then I must put aside my self-centered pride and *believe* what I hold as true — whether I am viewed as a fool or not. I must be as daring as Christ, the Apostles, and the martyrs. I must become a

---

[65] See 1 Corinthians 3:18.

person of both faith *and* hope, remembering that my hope is not without reason.

While some people will persist in thinking that there is no eternal life, and others will say that life after death cannot be patently proven or disproven, *Christians have seen the evidence.* Jesus Christ rose from the dead and ascended into Heaven. Eye-witnesses, who were too mindful to be lunatics and too brave in the face of death to be liars, testified to this far and wide, and their testimonies were recorded and handed on by likewise reliable people. Through the death and Resurrection of Christ, who is fully God and fully man, God has saved mankind from endless death. Ultimate resurrection and eternal life in Heaven is the promise that God Incarnate made to all of us who follow His way and believe.

Heaven is real. And the reality of Heaven necessarily adds a new dimension to the fact of death.

So, just as I seriously wondered as a teenager, let us wonder now: What will it be like to be dead?

Well, we can never be *fully dead.* Our bodies will no longer be able to hold onto life, they *will* die and decay back into the Earth, but the life of which the body lets go will continue. Our souls, which animate our bodies, are immortal and *cannot die.* So, the real question is, what will happen after our lungs stop breathing, our hearts stop beating, and our brains stop firing signals? What will *life* be like then?

My heart breaks for people who are so arrogantly unwilling to cling to anything but the material and to love anything but their own finite selves that, when face-to-face with eternity, they would blatantly refuse to humbly accept the reality of God's gracious existence and refuse to lovingly gaze into His infinite depths. What will happen to those who choose to turn away from God's merciful love in pride and hateful anger? Well, their experience of eternity, we are told and can well imagine, will be continued lives of their own torturous anger and self-centered hate, miserably hardened against receiving the saving mercy that pours out from God's broken heart.

Thanks be to the mercy of God, those who do not turn away from God's eternal mercy and love after bodily death, but who rather, on meeting their Maker, will run lovingly to Him who is their infinite Source, will find the inexpressible joy of Heaven ahead. Dying, then, for people of faith, does not only mean saying goodbye to our loved ones on Earth, but also preparing to say hello to heavenly bliss. The life of real love doesn't end but rather *continues in a new and amazing way.* There should be, I'm realizing as I mature, an excitement in this. It's terribly sad to have to leave this lovely life. I don't want to, but … what about the loveliness that awaits us on the other side in the life of the World to Come?

I don't believe that the hope of Heaven should cause us to think of Earth as solely a valley of tears, a land of exile that we want to flee for the sunnier shores of paradise. Rather, it is good and right to desire living now and to live our humanity *here*, because God wants us to embrace the earthly lives that He has given to us in the wondrous gift of His Creation. God desires us to live *fully*, body and soul, as the persons that He created us to be, knowing, loving, and serving all that is good, true, and beautiful as best as we can — mysteriously participating in the divine life *now* so that we can live its fulfillment forever. Baptized into Christ's life, death, Resurrection, and Ascension, our eternal lives have already begun, and they are being shaped by the way that we live and love in union with Christ *here and now*.

The abundant life that Jesus came to give us is meant to be lived abundantly *by* us through every stage and age, in sorrow and in delight, in sickness and in health, and even within the act of dying itself. No matter how long or short our dying courses may be, they, too, are to be embraced as part of life, as part of our *whole* lives, *our eternal lives*, for they are essential parts of our transitions from this world to the next. The physical transition is needed, just as a spiritual transition of purification (Purgatory) may be necessary for us to pass through the healing power of God's saving mercy into that glorious existence that we call Heaven—the unhindered joy of God's pure love.

When the Earth itself ultimately passes away, our mysteriously resurrected and glorified bodies will be united with our souls in that World that is undetectable to us now, the World that we have been promised, the World which we know of by faith and in which we have true hope. We will be fully alive in the life of that World to Come, our souls eternally animating our glorified bodies in its endless wonders and glory.

When the time of death comes for me and for you, that inevitable time when we can no longer continue our earthly lives, let our prayers be that we will not be so overcome with the sorrow of leaving that we forget the joyful excitement of arriving. Let us also pray that we will not be so overwhelmingly distraught when our loved ones leave this earthly life that we do not allow ourselves the consolation of *their* overwhelming joy in the life of Heaven.

The beauty and wonders that we experience now in the divine gift of the created world are a prelude and preparation, the seedlings and buds of the eternal garden of gorgeous grandeur, which is a mystery to us here. The Rockies and Alps are mere shadowy ridges compared to the endless, glorious vistas of pure Paradise. The delights of sunrises, wildflowers, kittens, and chocolate are trifling hints of the delights, wonders, enchantments, and beauties of God's unfiltered, unfettered realm. Even the love that we share with our families and friends—this magnificent love has always been a spiritual glimpse, whisper, and taste of the infinite and intimate love of our Divine Creator, the love in which we will be most gloriously and blissfully saturated and permeated, shining through, when we are fully in Heaven.

We are called to know this *now* and to live in this knowledge—to live eternal love—in hopeful *joy*.

Yes, there was a time when I thought that Heaven sounded like the kind of thing that you tell children. A fairy tale. But from whence do fairy tales come? Imagination? Yes, the human imagination is vibrantly amazing, but from whence does *it* come? Reduction to synapse flashes is not a worthy explanation of the fullness of reality, the fullness of being alive. It is God who has given us the gift of imagination so that we may be able to wonder, to seek, to try to understand, and to reach out to *Him*, to the fullness of what is real.

Every human being that is honest deeply desires an eternal state of being that is pure joy—Heaven. We need not be afraid of this desire, of this hope, because it has a corresponding reality, first imagined by God and then created for us. Heaven is our eternal *home*. Eternal life is real. We recognize this in faith and embrace it in hope, not without reason.

The blissful experience of Heaven, of unveiled eternal life and pure love, is far beyond all possible imagining, but maybe it doesn't hurt to try. We are creative creatures. Our delightful creativity is one of the gifts derived from being images of God, the Creator of Heaven and Earth, of all that is seen and unseen. Let us use our creative gifts, then, to imagine the unimaginable, to fathom an unfathomable glimpse of the Beatific Vision. And in the imagining, let us joyfully prepare ourselves for Heaven by living its reality here and now, by walking lovingly and generously in the way of Christ. Let us confidently ask God to guide us, so that we may be alive forever in the joy of His love.

I pray that when my time arrives to transition from this lovely Earth, whenever that will be, God will give me excitement for what is to come. May each of us be given the grace to hope, to anticipate the joy of Heaven, almost giddy with the imagining of all of its splendors and delights. Yes, like a child.

Like a child of God who's coming home.

Glorified Wounds: Suffer These Things and Enter into His Glory

Suffering wounds in our lives, we may wonder: why did Christ's wounds remain on His resurrected and glorified body?

It was not enough for God's loving plan of salvation that He should come amazingly, in awesome humility, among us, living fully as one of us, sanctifying every moment of human life, every aspect of being human, and teaching us all how to live the fullness of life through self-giving love. It was not even enough that God Incarnate should give Himself so completely to us in love, so painfully and profoundly to us, that He suffered the effects of our sins in His Passion, willingly offering Himself as a sacrifice in the language of atonement, thus putting to death the damages of sin. To fulfill the divine plan of salvation, Jesus also had to rise from the dead—*bodily*. He had to put Death itself beneath His feet—not only as God, who has sovereignty over everything, but also as a fragile human being, so that we, as human beings, may triumph over death, too, through Him.

The human body that is subject to death has been resurrected and glorified in Christ Jesus. Eternity does not belong to spirit only, but also to flesh. Praise be to God, *wondrous Mystery of Mysteries*.

However, it was not *precisely* Jesus's ordinary body that rose from the dead. Jesus's very human body became re-animated with life, not so that it may die again, but so that it may live forever. The life of Jesus's resurrected body is not the same kind of life that He knew before His death. His resurrected body is *glorified*, meaning that His body is fully alive in a special way and capable of doing amazing things that earthly, unglorified human bodies cannot do.

In His resurrected and glorified state, some of Jesus's close friends and disciples didn't recognize Him right away. There was something so changed in the quality of His flesh that He looked different. He still looked like a regular man; there was nothing disturbing or remarkable about His appearance, for Mary Magdalene even mistook Him for a gardener. And He was still identifiable as Himself, as evidenced by Mary recognizing Him once He spoke to her. When Jesus appeared to the disciples in the locked room, they thought that He was a ghost of Himself. But a ghost He was not, for He did not resurrect to exist as a spirit or as an apparition. He rose completely, body and soul. He urged His shocked disciples to grab hold of His arms, to feel His flesh and bones, and He even ate some food to reassure them.

We can also tell that Christ's glorified body was different because, bodily present though He was, He did physical things that He didn't do before. He passed through locked doors without opening them and appeared in spread out places at impossibly quick intervals of time (impossible in earthly terms). Most importantly, He was able to ascend into Heaven—to leave our earthly perception and, yet, to remain fully Himself.

Mysterious and powerful as Jesus's resurrected and glorified body was, the most profound beauty was that His wounds, the marks of His crucifixion, *were intact*. But why keep them?

When Jesus rose from the dead, the nail holes remained in His hands and His feet, and the cavity gaped open where His heart had been pierced. The apostle Thomas was invited to put his fingers into these very holes and his hand right into the open wound in Jesus's side. This is a bit bewildering to us, for we may think that, surely, Jesus's glorified body should be healed, whole, and without any blemish. Why would He be able to do miraculous things and yet not heal such disfigurement on His glorified body?

Surely, Jesus wouldn't want to carry His wounds with Him eternally into pure paradise?

But that's exactly what God Incarnate chose to do.

As creatures, we tend to judge by appearances, but God does not. Jesus knows that His terrible wounds are not ugly, but rather are the rare and precious gifts of Beauty itself. For the beautiful wholeness of Creation is bound together by God's self-giving love — God in the flesh would not have wounds at all unless He loved us and became one of us. Christ's wounds are borne in divine love — they are eternally powerful. The wounds are *sacred* and *blessed* because, through them, we, God's most beloved creatures, are *healed*, body, mind, heart, and soul. Christ healed us, not so that we may be without physical flaw, but so that we may be cleansed of division and united intimately and infinitely with God's perfect love. His wounds bind us together, God and man. For these reasons, Jesus lovingly carries His bodily wounds into paradise, glorified. He will also bring ours with Him to be glorified, blessedly sacred and beautiful.

Whenever reflecting upon the Alleluia awe of the Resurrection, let us tenderly ponder the precious wounds of Christ, glorified in Heaven. Let us see in them how much God loves us, utterly and unreservedly, and let us remember that each and every one of us is eternally beautiful in His eyes—wounds, scars, and all. Wounded though we may be, through divine mercy, through the humble and awestruck reception of divine love, we are made worthy to be glorified.

Weird and Wonderful: The Essence of the Ascension

The belief in the Ascension, and even in Heaven itself, may seem radical, weird, and even irrational to some. Christians profess that Jesus not only rose from the dead, but also went bodily to a supernatural place that we call Heaven. He did not symbolically ascend into a symbolic Heaven. This is a true account and a real place. Yes, weird. But true.

Christ's risen body is glorified, we believe, able to eat, walk, withstand probing, and all the other things that a normal body can do, but it's also able to pass through walls and bear a deadly wound without infection or bleeding. And now, Jesus, in all that He is, both human and divine, abides bodily ... somewhere ... some*where* that isn't *exactly here* or *there*. Somewhere from which He will return, somewhere that we hope to be.

This is the Christian Faith. And it does seem rather too fantastic to be true.

But then again ... have you heard about quarks? Dark matter? Dark energy? The world that we take to be solid and true is too wonderful to comprehend in its entirety or even in the entirety of its smallest part. (What *is* its smallest part?) We would know nothing of the existence of, say, subatomic particles, if a privileged few people hadn't "seen" them and then told us about them. Tales of white dwarfs and blackholes sound like mere tall tales, indeed, but the small percentage of our population called scientists are intelligent and fervent in their telling of them. And we accept. We have not seen the proof and, even if we did, most of us would not be able to understand the proof, but we profess that it is true.

Life is profoundly complex and marvelously *weird*. As intelligent as scientists may be, we would be arrogant to think that everything in existence can fit into our limited human brains — even their big scientific ones. There is much more to learn than what we know, than what we can possibly know in our finiteness; there is much more than what we can even imagine.

The myriad clusters of stars and sweeps of galaxies in the night sky are as beautiful to my eyes as the similarly exuberant profusion of blue forget-me-nots in the garden beneath my window. Sometimes, we may think that the superabundance of suns and planets in the universe renders the specially intended and divinely loved existence of human beings into a myth. And yet is it a myth, a fairy tale, that the superabundance of apple blossoms rarely yields forth another fruit-producing tree? From twelve thousand seeds come not twelve thousand plants. All that is needed, all that we might even hope for, is but *one*. But one is precious and worth the extravagance. From that one tiny seed will flourish a symphony of life.

This is the way that God creates. And this is how God creates because this is how God *loves* — profusely, lavishly, excessive in creative exuberance and abundant mercy. What goodness we experience now is only the smallest part of what *will* be.

So, yes. I believe. Jesus, Our Savior and Lord, is fully where He promised to be, where He will call us to join Him one day.

Although we may not know "where" that is, we know the way, which is pure and generously self-giving love without ceasing. Just so, though we may not understand the exact workings of the copious stars and flowers, we fully know the beauty — the wonder and awe-inspiring beauty of life *loved* exuberantly into being.

The Assumption and Every Body

There are cemeteries all over the world, holding the mortal remains of billions of human beings — a reminder that our time on this Earth is limited. Perhaps you, like me, live near the cemetery where your grandparents are buried, or maybe your parents or sibling, a friend, a spouse, or your own child. Traditionally, in most Christian cemeteries, all of the bodies were buried facing toward the east, the direction of the rising sun and the new day, in anticipation of the end of days when all of earthly life will come to its inevitable end and we will experience the General Resurrection in the World to Come.[66] Their mortal remains have been interred by their loved ones, with reverent prayers, in hopes that they will see them again, resurrected, soul and glorified body reunited, in the eternity of Heaven.

Of course, the body of Jesus Christ is not buried anywhere because He rose from the dead, His body glorified, and He ascended into Heaven. However, the deceased bodies of holy Christian men and women, the simple and unremembered saints on Earth as well as the canonized saints, are buried in tombs and cemeteries

[66] See Matthew 24:27–31.

throughout the nations. We can even go visit their graves or honor their relics. These mortal remains of the saints are lying in wait for the resurrection, just like the remains of the people buried in your local cemetery, beneath the green lawn.

But ...

Where is the Virgin Mary buried?

If you can't think of the answer to that question, it's because there is no "where." The very definition of the Catholic Church's dogma of the Assumption of the Blessed Virgin Mary states, "The Immaculate Mother of God, the ever Virgin Mary, having completed the course of her earthly life, was assumed body and soul into heavenly glory."[67]

This belief was held by early Christians in both the East and the West. In the Eastern traditions of the Catholic Church, the "Dormition" of Mary has been officially celebrated as a Holy Day on August 15 for nearly 1,400 years, following even more ancient beliefs of the faithful. Because of this deeply rooted tenet of faith, as is written in the document defining the dogma of the Assumption, "the Church has never looked for the bodily relics of the Blessed Virgin nor proposed them for the veneration of the people."[68] In other words, there is no grave, known or unknown, no tomb, no reliquary holding the mortal remains of the Blessed Virgin Mary because *nothing mortal of the Blessed Virgin Mary remains.*

If Jesus Christ is God Incarnate, then it is absolutely appropriate that He rose bodily from the dead, His body glorified, and then ascended into heavenly glory. Christ is fully human, sharing our

---

[67] Pius XII, Apostolic Constitution *Munificentissimus Deus* (November 1, 1950), no. 44.

[68] Ibid., no. 33.

human nature, but He is also fully divine, being God-made-man, after all. But by believing that Christ's mother, too, was assumed bodily into Heaven, what are we saying about her? Mary isn't God. She's a human person like us, daughter of both a human mother and a human father, with no divine nature at all. Why, then, aren't her earthly remains lying somewhere, like those in the local cemetery, like those of the other saints, awaiting the end of days and the General Resurrection?

By virtue of her being Christ's own mother — *Theotokos*, God-bearer, the Mother of God — God gave the Blessed Virgin Mary special graces and privileges from the instant of her creation (her Immaculate Conception) through the natural end of her earthly life. She who gave herself completely to divine will, saying to the angel of God, "May it be done to me according to your word,"[69] conceived, carried, birthed, and nursed Our Lord. From her human flesh, God's Word was made flesh, and therefore she was granted the privilege of not suffering any decomposition of the flesh or the corruption of the tomb. In other words, she didn't have to wait until the end of days for "the resurrection of the body and life everlasting."[70] This is her unique and holy privilege, by the grace of God.

Imagine what it was like when Mary's earthly life came to a close, at the time of her "Dormition," as the Eastern Churches call it. When the Assumption actually took place, I imagine that it was a very intimate event, private, loving, between a mother and a Son. This aged woman, the beloved mother of our Savior, closed her earthly eyes for the last time and, by the tender grace of God, opened her glorified eyes to eternity, her much-loved body and soul intact in precious union.

[69] Luke 1:38.
[70] Apostles' Creed.

Over the centuries, the reality of the Assumption has become for us, more and more, a tremendous hope and a crucial reminder. She, who is a human person, now shares *bodily* in the divine life for all eternity—the salvation and glory that is offered to each and every one of us through Christ our Lord. Mary, as the New Eve, the Mother of all the living in Christ, went before us, and we hope to follow at the end of time. That is the hope that every cemetery and every grave encloses.

The Assumption was declared dogma by the Catholic Church in 1950, putting an official stamp and explanation on what Christians have believed for two millennia. We may wonder why it took so long for the declaration to be made, but we know that all things happen in God's time. There was indeed profound timing involved in this dogma, so that we will never forget that *matter* matters to God. The proclamation came forth just after World War II, an atrocious period of history when millions of human beings were systematically murdered, having been stripped and gassed, their dead bodies heaped in piles like cordwood. Technology allowed the graphic images of this massacre and desecration to spread, and the world was horrified by them.

And the Church took action.

With the proclamation of the dogma of the Assumption of the Blessed Virgin Mary, the Universal Church, founded by our Lord and Savior Jesus Christ, gave us a powerful reminder of the unassailable dignity and divine destiny of every human person—body and soul.

Our bodies are sacred and essential to who we are, not some kind of prison from which the soul has to escape or some meaningless shell that we can do with as we wish. We are created by God as creatures of both flesh and spirit—*body and soul as one person*—and we believe that our souls will be reunited with our glorified bodies at the end of time. Therefore, it is right and just to respect the body. God loves what He has created. The human body is created by God and is not to be profaned, mutilated, abused, murdered, or desecrated in any way—for *every* human being is loved by God and divinely intended for perfection, soul *and* body, in the fulfillment of heavenly glory.

Perhaps, you have seen someone as deformed as I am, with my severe scoliosis, my head flopped over to rest on my hunchback, or someone who is even more misshapen, someone hideously disfigured. Maybe one of your loved ones is suffering from severe mental illness, Alzheimer's disease, or extreme autism or brain injury, causing behavior that is sorrowfully distressing or even shocking. You may have heard of someone or have a friend, coworker, neighbor, or family member who lives an unwholesome life, who seems to you to be terribly far from the ideal of a human person, who may even seem to you to be inferior in some way. Let us remember how Christ treated His fellow human beings. He lovingly reached out and touched the lepers. He had tender mercy on those who were called demoniacs. And He sat and dined with those considered irredeemable sinners. Christ did these things because He *loves* human beings.

God loves us so much that He became one of us, His little body developing in total dependency on His mother's womb and growing through infancy into adulthood, active and resting, experiencing both pleasure and pain. Jesus Christ, God in the flesh, loves His fellow human beings so much that He willingly gave His life intimately and completely for humankind, enabling each and every person to experience the divine life of love and be redeemed to the beautiful eternal destiny that He sees waiting for them.

It's Good to Be Here

We know that human beings come in all physical shapes and sizes and with all levels of physical and mental abilities. Some of us have twisted or missing limbs and some have faces so scarred or disfigured that they are hardly recognizable as human. Far too often, in our society, we don't even recognize human beings in the first stages of their lives because they can't do what society declares human beings are supposed to be able to do. Make no mistake about it: whether tiny or incapable, whether impaired in cognition or mobility, whether slowed or drooling, whether deformed or aged and decrepit, *we are all living humans*. And if we are truly going to live in the fullness of being human, then we must remember that everybody, *every body*, is beautiful in the eyes of God, who alone sees our eternal glory — the glory for which He created each and every one of us in loving union with Him.

What would happen if we could glimpse each other's future heavenly glory? What if we truly remembered that each human creature we encounter, whether developing, diseased, healthy, mentally disabled, physically deformed, or mired in sin, is *exquisitely beautiful* in the eternal eyes of God? If we could see the resplendent glory that *God intends*, now and forever, for each one of them — for each one of us — *we would be blown away* by the intense radiance of that beauty, the eternal destiny of every human being redeemed and resurrected by the power of God's love.

Maybe, just maybe, we would then love one another as God loves us, with respect, forgiveness, patience, affection, and generosity, seeing ourselves and our fellow human beings as God sees us in the loving gift of life that He has given us and the eternal glory that He has in store for us. And then maybe we would experience something of Heaven in our limited time on Earth.

Holy Mary, Blessed Virgin, Mother of God, and all of the angels and saints who are now in perfect loving union with Christ, pray for us to the Lord our God so that the eyes of our hearts may be open to perceive the heavenly resplendence and divinely loved beauty of everybody.

7

I Will Be with You Always

On Christ's Ever-Presence:
My Personal Encounters with Christ
in the Liturgy, the Sacraments, People,
and the Created World

Good News

I once had a cancer scare. The fear of dying of such a dreaded disease renewed in me the understanding of earthly life's transient nature. It wasn't as though the thought of dying young was new to me, since my genetic disease means that I will not be able to live a long life. But thinking of something so pointed in its targeting of life as cancer made me, very quickly, want to live without the wasting of a single moment or a single gift. It also made me turn to more intense prayer, of course.

Why do we seem to need fear to bring us deeper into our relationship with God? I prayed that God would allow only His perfect, positive, holy, ordained will to be done to me. I prayed that I might be healed and spared from cancer, but also that I be given the grace and courage to accept God's will, whatever that was, and to live and die as the person that God created me to be.

Then, one Sunday, as I was heading out of church, I knew. I was healed.

It didn't come like a bolt out of the blue or a disembodied voice, or like some televangelist with his palm on my forehead saying the words. I just knew. After Mass and some friendly conversations, somewhere between my mental genuflection before the tabernacle and crossing the threshold out into the world, my worries and prayers concerning whether or not I had cancer had an answer—"I am healed."

I was filled with a light, clear brightness, like a many-colored stained-glass window radiant with sun. This wasn't merely a pleasant feeling; it was more of a deep-down knowledge. Later, as I prayed the Glorious Mysteries of the Holy Rosary at home, I again experienced the awareness and was brought to tears of joy.

Even when I thought about how healing has different meanings, that this knowledge of mine might not mean that I was cancer-free, I still had a sense of peace. I knew that I was healed, and that meant something. Maybe it meant that I was healed of my fears and my wariness of hope. Maybe it meant that I would have a peaceful, joyful, and inspiring transition into the next life. I didn't know for certain. I just knew that I was healed.

My worry had gotten so bad that I had called my doctor to get an earlier appointment, wanting to get the test done and over with so that I would know whether the tumors were benign or malignant. After that Sunday's experience, however, I didn't feel the same anxiety at all. I wasn't anxious. I was healed. Knowing myself, however, I knew that it wouldn't take much for me to lose the sense of peace and start to worry again. (How God puts up with me, I don't know.) Also, the thought that my parents might be worried, too, did come to mind. So, I went for the earlier test and received good news: no cancer.

Perhaps, it was a miracle—I think it was. *Alleluia!*

But I also know that if the test had shown that I did have terminal cancer and I had gracefully accepted it, then that would have been a miracle, too. I already know something of the miracle of acceptance. *Bless the Lord, O my soul, for He has done wonderful things!*

All of this caused me to reflect upon the Good News.

My experience on that Sunday after Mass, when I knew that I was healed, began to open up my heart and mind to Sunday itself—to the intent of the liturgy, the meaning of salvation, and the reason for the Gospel, a word that translates to "good news." I started thinking that everyone should leave Mass knowing that they are healed. I should have been experiencing this awareness all along because, all along, I had been healed. I am being healed. I am healed. We all are. That is the Good News of the Gospel—Christ Jesus came to bring us forgiveness of our sinful faults and failings and eternal reconciliation with our Creator and all Creation: the merciful fruit of God's saving love. By and through Christ, we are healed and restored to the joy of paradisiacal living in union with the Divine.

The Apostles essentially went around Jerusalem and throughout the whole world proclaiming, "You are healed! You are healed!" Those who believed them, those who came to faith in Jesus their Healer, their Savior, lived their earthly lives with the heavenly peace of unity with Christ, lovingly proclaiming the good news to others, and, in death, passed confidently and joyfully into God's pure and eternal embrace. This is the Good News.

This is the Gospel proclaimed to us every Sunday.

Because of the Paschal Mystery, sanctifying grace is available to all, enabling us creatures to participate in the divine life. Being both human and divine, Jesus Christ's gift of Himself in loving sacrifice—in which we are present and connected through the Eucharistic Liturgy of every Mass—pours out abundant grace to us in the ultimate healing power of divine mercy and love, uniting us with God now and forever. This vital gift is signified by and received through the sacraments of the Church.

Baptized into the life, death, and resurrection of Christ, we are born anew of water and Spirit[71]—we are new creations living supernaturally. The Holy Spirit is given to us to dwell and work within us, and the gifts of the Spirit of God bear fruit through us into the world, through the work of Christ's love that makes firm the Spirit within us. When we fail to live up to the divine image in which we have been created, when we become blind, deaf, and crippled by sin, the Spirit within us prompts our repentance, and our sincere penitence allows Christ to heal us so that we may again see and hear His goodness and walk in His way. Christ nourishes us with His Body, Blood, Soul, and Divinity, giving us the spiritual strength and sustenance that we need to be transformed more and more into Him. Answering God's particular call to us to live holy lives, we receive actual grace to fulfill our vocations as images of God, so that Christ may lead us and walk with us in our missions to bring the Good News to a world in need of healing. Even when we are sick, even at the end of our earthly lives, Christ is with us, powerfully, through the holy anointing of the sacrament of the sick and dying, to accomplish the healing that is the Good News of reconciliation and eternal life within us.

All of the sacraments offer us actual grace and, with it, the healing power of God directly into our lives, here and now.

And, so, *we are healed.*

Too often, however, especially when we are troubled by sorrow or suffering, we don't even know it.

But whether we are conscious of it or not, we *are* truly healed. We are healed! Alleluia!

> *My Lord and my God, have mercy on me.*
> *Help me to always live the Good News.*

[71] See John 3:5.

Sitting in the Back and the Real Presence

I am very much aware that the Catholic belief about the Eucharist seems strange to many, like superstitious nonsense at best and blasphemy at worst. Do we Catholics really believe that the consecrated bread and wine of Holy Communion has become the Body and Blood of Jesus Christ? Yes, we do. Not symbolically. Really. *Truly*.

We don't believe that we are eating an ear or a foot or anything irrational like that, but that Christ Jesus *is* really present in the Eucharist, *substantially* present, sacramentally present — you could maybe say spiritually present, but *not* symbolically present. We believe that we are eating the flesh and drinking the blood of the Son of Man, just like Jesus tells us in the Gospel of St. John[72] and because of what the Apostles have handed down to us in Scripture and Tradition — the teachings of Christ safeguarded by the Holy Spirit.

The firmly rooted tenet that the consecrated bread and wine is the Body, Blood, Soul, and Divinity of Jesus Christ *is* difficult to believe, however. Frankly, there are many Catholics who have to say, "Lord, I believe! Help my unbelief!"[73]

---

[72] John 6:51–57.
[73] See Mark 9:24.

It's Good to Be Here

I'm not quite sure if I would even be able to say to God that I believe (for God sees the truth of my heart better than I do) if it hadn't been for one blessed day ...

Having rediscovered my given Catholic Faith as a young adult and intentionally choosing Christ for myself, I became a new Christian, a faithful member of the mystical Body of Christ, His Church—a born-again Catholic, if you will. The blessed day of Eucharistic faith came when my life as a committed Christian was still young, and I was just beginning to go to Mass every Sunday that I felt well enough to do so. (I was nearly thirty.) In fact, I had only begun physically attending Mass every week in order to pray for our pastor, who had just taken a leave of absence due to personal difficulties. On his last day in our church, he had knelt down beside me and had asked me to pray for him. I can't tell you how many times people have looked at me in my wheelchair and asked me to pray for them, believing me to be better at it than I am because of my physical suffering. Still, I decided to overlook any prejudice on his part, and, knowing that he needed the prayers, I allowed the Holy Spirit to work within me and made the decision to truly *do* something for this man in his sacred vocation as God's priest. I decided that I would physically push my weak and nervous self to go to Mass every Sunday—even when tired, even when queasy—and offer the labor as a sacrifice in union with Christ's love on the Cross for this priest's benefit.

The particular Sunday of my blessed experience with the Eucharist was the First Communion celebration in our parish, a Mass that I usually didn't push to attend because of the overcrowding and my uneasiness with unfamiliar routines. My wheelchair only fits next to the first two rows of pews or behind the very last one in the back. Since the first pews are reserved for the children and their families during First Communion, and the Mass can be quite long and tiring, I usually stayed at home and participated in the Eucharistic Liturgy through a televised broadcast from Boston.

Not that day.

Due to my intentions for the suffering priest, I went with my mother and sat in the rear of the church behind the last pew. Situated in that spot, when I returned to my place in the back after receiving Holy Communion, I was alone, with no one looking at me.

For once, at church, I wasn't self-conscious. Too many times in my life I have been beset by crippling self-consciousness, related, perhaps, to the sin of self-centeredness and self-absorption. However, that day, with the Communion wafer in my mouth, I was completely relaxed and at ease with myself in the dim silence, with no one to look at me and no prideful need for my pseudo-fig leaves. There was just me. Just me ... and ... and ...

I remember biting into the consecrated bread with my teeth and being completely struck with the awareness of the Real Presence. Alone and silent, the core of my being took over, and I was thinking of how God became human for me and how God Incarnate wants me to gnaw upon His flesh.[74] He wants to feed me with His very self; He wants to give Himself totally and completely to me, Body, Blood, Soul, and Divinity. "O *sublime humility!*"[75] My eyeteeth pierced through the Body of Christ as did the nails on the Cross, and I was overwhelmed. I wept, unmindful of the tears.

God comes to me in the Most Blessed Sacrament so that I may consume Him, and in that moment, as I humbly received

[74] See John 6:57.
[75] St. Francis of Assisi, *Letter to All the Friars.*

the Body of Christ into my own body, in wonder and awe, *I was consumed* by His love.

For almost a year afterward, I silently cried after receiving Christ in Holy Communion. I would always be embarrassed, with the tears falling down my face and my disease-weakened hands unable to wipe them away, but I was willing for God to do with me whatsoever He willed. It was such a gift. Those were such moments of grace, such blessings, for it is a rarity when we experience a heart-mind-body understanding of what we believe in our souls.

Those moments didn't last. I knew that they wouldn't. It is not God's will for us to always *feel* Him, to regularly experience, with the fullness of our senses and intellect, His Divine Presence. If we were forever in those deep and heightened moments of ecstasy, we could not function as creatures of this earth.

God put us here for a reason. And the reason is not to *feel* good. The reason is to *be* good, to be *goodness*, as images of God in His beloved and good Creation. "Because you have seen me, you have believed; blessed are those who have not seen and yet have believed."[76] Jesus told this to Thomas because there is something more beautiful and powerful than physical experience and informational knowledge—and that is *faith*. I believe in the astonishing depths of God's love. Perhaps I am no longer weeping in awe and experiencing the feeling of joyful love every time I receive Christ in the Eucharist, but I am—body, mind, heart, and soul—gratefully leaping in faith.

[76] John 20:29.

Well Done, Good and Faithful Servant

Think about what it was like for those privileged few who actually got to know Jesus in His earthly life, conversing, eating, and living with Him. What an unimaginable joy that must have been to actually know Christ in the flesh, being able to laugh with Him and cry with Him, to embrace Him and be embraced by Him. As people of faith, we believe that we will, by the mercy of God, see Christ face-to-face in Heaven and experience the wonder and awe of person-to-person encounter with Our Lord.

But do we really have to wait until after we are dead to have such a personal and intimate encounter with God? This supernatural experience — is it only relegated to the heavenly realm and barred from the earthly?

Oh, no. God, in His great love and generosity, enables us to experience His presence here and now in our earthly lives in many ways. Through deep and reverent prayer, we are able to have communication with Our Lord and know that He is sorrowing with us, rejoicing with us, and giving us His wisdom and strength to lean upon always. He instructs and informs us through His presence in Sacred Scripture and tells us that, wherever two or more of us are gathered in His name, there He is in our midst. We receive His presence substantially and intimately through the holy sacraments, as He pours His own life within us, heals us, and guides us ever closer to His divine will, through words heard and spoken by His priests and through very earthly things like water and oil. In the holy Sacrifice of the Mass, Christ is again present among us, giving Himself completely to us, as we receive Him, Body, Blood, Soul, and Divinity beneath the very solid appearance of bread and wine.

This is profoundly beautiful and powerful. There is infinite goodness and mercifully divine graciousness in this. But …

But we still long for more. We want to *see* Him, and the wondrous artwork that our human hands render to depict Our Lord is not enough. Even those moments when we are submerged in prayerful depths and glimpse something of the divine in our hearts … we often come out of those moments wanting to see and *touch* God bodily. Living as persons of both soul and body, we want to encounter God Incarnate in our everyday actions, *living among us here and now.*

Perhaps, this is natural. Perhaps, this is exactly what God intends.

God wants us to desire His presence in the flesh and puts this desire in our hearts because He wants us to seek Him in the world, in our daily lives, and is waiting for us, *needing us,* to find Him and to minister personally to Him.

We are created to know, love, and serve God in *this* life, and to serve God doesn't only mean obeying His commandments and sharing the Gospel with others, but also literally *serving Him.* When you make a sandwich for someone who is hungry, you are serving that sandwich to God in the flesh. When you give a glass of water to someone who is parched, you are giving refreshment to Christ Himself. We know that all of the ways of encountering Christ in our world are divinely sacred, holy, and very, very good — liturgies are sublimely beautiful, Sacred Scripture is eloquent and meaningful, and the holy sacraments of the Church and the prayers of our hearts are awe-inspiring and powerfully effective — but holding a bucket for someone who is sick and vomiting is sublimely beautiful, eloquent, and awe-inspiring, too. Its divine goodness and power are effective because that person *is Christ* who is wretchedly ill, and you are there to make Him feel a little better.

Christ Jesus said, "For I was hungry and you gave me food, I was thirsty and you gave me drink, a stranger and you welcomed me, naked and you clothed me, ill and you cared for me, in prison and you visited me."[77] When He spoke these words recorded in St. Matthew's Gospel,[78] Jesus meant to be provocative. He took our misconception of lordship as " lording over" and flipped it on its head, intentionally provoking wonder and awe at His profound unity and identity with every suffering human being for all time.

God Incarnate tells us that whatever we do for the least ones among us, we do for Him. This declaration is not symbolic, but rather a very real, mysterious connection between us and Christ. God is with us, here and now. Jesus is waiting for us to greet Him and to care for Him in the flesh. Let us not miss the sacred privilege of eating, drinking, and conversing with Him right here, of comforting Him, cleaning up after Him, and embracing Him right now. Oh, the sacred wonder of every blessed human relationship — every one is a mysteriously direct encounter with Almighty God.

To live this blessed truth is an awesome gift and privilege, a divinely wonderful understanding of reality and of the intimate

[77] Matthew 25:35–36.
[78] See Matthew 25:31–46.

love God has for us and we for Him, but it's also a serious challenge and an acute responsibility. If we are capable of helping
another in need and choose not to help, then we fail terribly in
the way of what is good, true, and beautiful. We fail Christ. Jesus
said, "I was hungry and you gave me no food, I was thirsty and you
gave me no drink, a stranger and you gave me no welcome, naked
and you gave me no clothing, ill and in prison, and you did not
care for me."[79] Anybody who has the ability to feed, clothe, or
care for people in need and turns a blind eye and deaf ear to their
suffering, anybody whose ability to help or welcome is paralyzed
through laziness, fear, or greed, is missing out on meeting *Christ
Himself* and having an intimate relationship with God on Earth.

How many times have we walked right past Jesus? If this makes
you feel a little guilty, then join the club. The human club. I'm
still haunted by the memory of an old beggar whom I passed by
outside of a church without even giving him a kind look. We all
miss opportunities to minister to Christ. We all miss the mark;
we are all weak in the flesh, even if willing in spirit. But Christ
forgives the repentant, and every day brings new occasions to ask
God to send His Holy Spirit to open our eyes and ears to Christ's
presence among us and to strengthen and guide our feet toward
His suffering self in the world.

No one of us is able to minister to everybody in need, but
each one of us is called to help the people that we can, with the
loving understanding that, in them, we are experiencing the solid
presence of Jesus here and now, chatting with Him and eating
with Him, consoling and comforting Him. With our particular
strengths, abilities, and talents, we are called to do what we are
able to do for those in need of love and care.

[79] Matthew 25:42–43.

One person may be able to use his plentiful and obvious resources to help build homes for the homeless or provide emergency aid for those starving in the midst of drought or war, thus sheltering and feeding Christ. Another person may be able to use her amazing gift for persuasion to right wrongs in oppressive countries, or to procure medicine to help bring relief and comfort to those who are diseased or dying, thus ministering to God Incarnate. Most of us, with simpler means and talents, can volunteer at a soup kitchen, visit someone in a nursing home or prison, bring groceries to a neighbor who has lost his job, help an ailing person home, or dry the tears of a child. Through any and every act of real kindness, we will meet and love Christ in the flesh.

Even if a person is severely limited in strengths and abilities through some kind of impairment, he or she can still personally encounter and minister to Our Lord in ministering to others. Little things done with great love are the greatest gifts that we can give directly to God, like waiting for assistance with patience and understanding, then smiling kindly at caregivers with appreciation, or like remarking upon the beauty of someone's eyes or voice, or noticing the worry across someone's face. By listening with deep sympathy to the cares and concerns of others, even when we ourselves may be suffering from some burden, we are listening as we might like to have listened to Our Lord when He was under sorrow and strain. When we do this, when we give a compassionate ear to someone who is upset or sad, we are weeping with Chris; we are letting Him rest His head upon us as we hold His hand.

What every person can do, even someone who is in a vegetative state, is intimately participate in *God's love*. Even if unable to communicate with or cognitively understand the outside world, all human beings, at every stage of development and in every walk of life, are personal images of God in intimate union with Christ. In receiving loving care from others, they are enabling those others to encounter the Divine.

God knows I have very few abilities, as my crippling disease prevents me from even giving a hug. I'm the one that needs somebody to feed me, clothe me, and care for me. I've been told often enough, however, that my mere appreciation and joy for being alive is a powerful inspiration. Sometimes we can provide a glimpse, a brief encounter with Christ for others, without even intending it. "Your smile is exactly what I needed today," a man once told me, "because I've been feeling overburdened and discouraged all week." This stranger did look lighter and more radiant when he said these words to me than when I had first caught sight of him.

Understanding the sacred wonder of every human interaction, we can become immersed in the divine presence even in the simplest of moments. Take as an example the day that my dad and I were passing through the bright and lofty lobby of a medical center when we saw a woman in chains.

There were two deputy sheriffs beside her, badges and guns clearly visible, escorting her toward the soaring, glass-enclosed exit. She was obviously a prisoner, clothed in an orange jumpsuit, either a convicted criminal or someone awaiting trial without bail. She must have needed some kind of medical attention that the prison or jail could not provide. Shackles and guns would make sure that she wouldn't elude the law and escape. And as we neared each other, heading in opposite directions, I decided exactly what I wanted to do.

You see, having noticed her, I was going to have to do *something* with her. Whatever I did after noticing her would be a *response to her*, a response to her entrance into a brief moment of my life. This is how interaction with human beings works. We are not created to move about in vacuums of irrelevance to each other. I had to make a choice: to ignore and dismiss her; to stare at her or to blatantly avoid looking at her; to make a comment, crass or kind, to or about her; to chat with my father as if I hadn't seen her; or to say nothing at all.

We are continually encountering strangers and making decisions regarding them, sometimes more consciously than others. This is not something that we usually keep in mind — or perhaps are even aware of — when we are going out to an office, restaurant, store, or church, but it's definitely something that we do. We notice, and we react.

So, *how* should we react?

I reacted to the prisoner the same way that I would react to a dirty-looking homeless person, a scary-looking tough guy, a feeble-looking elder, or a young and beautiful child. It was an intentional reaction, emboldened by the Holy Spirit, yielding what I have come to understand as one of the greatest powers that has been given to me.

I made eye contact with the prisoner, and I smiled at her as we passed.

Were you expecting more?

We are all given gifts, tremendous or tiny, that have the power to change other people's lives in small but substantial ways. I would not, however, have chosen my own powerful gift to be a crooked little smile atop a crooked little body. But like it or not, that's how God has seen fit to show forth to others the divine peace and joy that His love brings, to let them know that they are loved. This is how God has chosen to work His minor miracles through me — *if I let Him*. Hardened hearts can soften to compassion, jaded eyes can open to unexpected beauty, and sorrowful burdens can lighten to perspective and gratitude in the radiance of God's love — a glimpse of which shines through my genuine smile. The renewing, educating, or heartening effect of such a little act of love is subtle, of course, and probably only temporary. I can't even know when my heartfelt smile does any good at all. It doesn't always work to soften, open, and lighten, of course, because people aren't always ready and willing to receive the love that God is perpetually, eternally giving them.

In looking over at the prisoner that day in order to see one of God's beloved children (for that's the first thing that we need to recognize about every person that we encounter), I had seen that she was about thirty years old, medium build, with dark brown hair and dark eyes. Pretty ordinary looking, even in the context of orange suit, chains, badges, and guns. I had a bit of difficulty looking her in the eye, but only because I had to force my eyeballs a little painfully up and to the left due to the awkward angle of my flopped over head on my crippled body. However, I did not have to try to get her attention in order to make eye contact with her because, I soon realized, she was already looking at me.

Of course she was. I was the other human being that stuck out oddly in the place. She was bound by the law, with heavy metal shackles on hand and foot; I was bound by disease, crumpled up in a mechanized wheelchair. We saw each other in a moment and the look on her face was actually a kind of pleasant one. There may have even been something almost like a smile about her face. She didn't look tough or scary, or even angry or sad. She looked ... almost kind? Perhaps, she was intentionally looking kindly at me as I was intentionally looking kindly at her.

Perhaps, we both saw Christ that day. Perhaps, we both *were* Christ in that brief, passing moment.

That is the sacred wonder of God in the flesh. Through God's lovingly generous assumption of humanity, humanity is given the gift of divine life here and now, as well as forever in glory. Do we fully embrace it? Do we receive?

Before Jesus ascended into Heaven, He said to those who loved Him, "And behold, I am with you always."[80] He *is* with us always, *everywhere*. We need only to look in order to see. The question is: do we look for Him?

Remember Jesus also told His disciples that not everyone who says to Him "Lord, Lord" will enter into Heaven. He may very well say to them, *to us*, "I never knew you."[81]

How will Christ know us after death if we never truly sought Him during life?

In order to have a real relationship with God, to know, love, and serve Him, it is not enough to *not* kill, to *not* commit adultery, and to *not* steal. Our lives shouldn't be about what we *don't* do as much as what we *do*. Yes, we should strive to avoid sin as much as humanly possible, but, in so doing, we should also strive to *seek Christ*. Let's not fail to see Christ here and now in our family members, our caregivers, our friends, our neighbors, our colleagues, strangers on the street, and even in the people that we don't like very much. We will truly love God in the flesh, here and now, by finding Him and loving Him in every person that needs love.

Every person needs love.

We may not live in first-century Palestine, but Jesus walks among us, waiting for us to acknowledge Him, to smile at Him, to embrace Him. He is ill, He is lonely, He is scared, and He is

---

[80] Matthew 28:20.
[81] Matthew 7:21–23.

desiring for us to take care of Him, to laugh with Him, and to cry with Him, to hold Him and minister to His needs—to love Him.

Yes, right there—do you see Him? There is Christ the Lord—there is God, Creator and Master of the Universe, who became a human being to live with us and love with us eternally.

He is *here*.

He is needing and waiting for you, right now.

The Strawberry and the Sacred Heart of Jesus

At the age of thirty-nine, on the Solemnity of Christ, King of the Universe, I made a personal act of consecration to the Sacred Heart of Jesus. My desire was to grow in *faith* but not without *reason*. The quest of a Christian is for the *whole* of reality, so I dedicated my life to the Sacred Heart because I love what God has created, and I want to love God through *all* that He has created, more and more. To me, in my particular understanding, which is in keeping with theological definitions, the Sacred Heart of Jesus is the Sacred Heart of Reality.

I first came closest to grasping this wonderful mystery while reflecting upon a strawberry. Yes, a little strawberry. The delightful and powerful revelation began with two very human questions.

Why Does Anything Exist?

As we read in the first chapter of the book of Genesis, God spoke His Word, and all of life, all of created reality, came into existence. God did not create the universe to be a personless cacophony of gaseous spheres solidifying and fleshy organisms evolving. No. God created the universe and brought all life into being for *love*. And love is not personless. Love is personal. Love is self-giving. God is love.

Creation is divinely created and loved by God, who looks upon it and sees that it is good. Likewise, human beings are divinely created and loved by God, infused with spiritual souls—as *persons*—to receive God's love and to love God, as well as to love Creation and one another as fellow creatures in the image of God. The giving and receiving of *love*, then, is the purpose and, therefore, the *joy* of Creation, the light that the darkness cannot overcome.[82]

Jesus is Love Incarnate, fully human and fully divine, with a divine nature and a human nature. He loves as both God and man. The Sacred Heart of Jesus, then, is where divine love and human love abide in perfect giving and receiving, in intimate unity, beating as one. This is the fulfillment of life, the hope of the universe, *the heart of reality*. In the presence of Jesus, even the stones rejoice![83]

What Is Truth? (*Who* Is Truth?)

In the Bible, we read of Christ as the life-giving Word of God made flesh, the Divine Word Incarnate, through whom all things were made. The order of creation is the truth of reality, and Christ is *Truth* Incarnate. Sublimely, we see Christ as the living heart of reality:

> In the beginning was the Word,
> and the Word was with God,
> and the Word was God.
> He was in the beginning with God.

[82] See John 1:5.
[83] Luke 19:40.

All things came to be through him,
and without him nothing came to be.
What came to be through him was life,
and this life was the light of the human race;
the light shines in the darkness,
and the darkness has not overcome it.…
And the Word became flesh
and made his dwelling among us,
and we saw his glory,
the glory as of the Father's only Son,
full of grace and truth.[84]

St. Paul speaks of the divine nature and personhood of Jesus when he says, "For in him dwells the whole fullness of the deity bodily."[85] The Apostle to the Gentiles also shows us Christ as the heart, the reason, *the meaning*, of reality: "All things were created through him and for him." He is the firstborn of all Creation and also the firstborn of the dead.[86] As Christ is the Word of God, through whom all things were made, He is also the saving Word of redemption, through whom the fallen away are reconciled to God, the truth of reality. He is "the Alpha and the Omega, the first and the last, the beginning and the end."[87]

We can easily imagine Jesus the man, flesh and blood, with a mom, friends, and a mission from God. We love this good man, this gentle, compassionate, and wise man, and we are grateful for His sacrifice for love of us and amazed by His resurrection. But how often do we think of Him as a *Divine Person*?

---

[84] John 1:1–5; 14.
[85] Colossians 2:9.
[86] See Colossians 1:15–20.
[87] Revelation 22:13.

If we believe in the Holy Trinity, then we know (if not fully understanding how) that Jesus is the second *Divine Person*, truly God, God the Son, who became a man. He is the Divine Word, the Word of God by which all of Creation came into being.

Let us try, then, to imagine our beloved Jesus speaking to us in these lines of Sacred Scripture:

> The LORD begot me, the beginning of his works,
> the forerunner of his deeds of long ago;
> From of old I was formed,
> at the first, before the earth.
> When there were no deeps I was brought forth,
> when there were no fountains or springs of water;
> Before the mountains were settled into place,
> before the hills, I was brought forth;
> When the earth and the fields were not yet made,
> nor the first clods of the world.
> When he established the heavens, there was I,
> when he marked out the vault over the face of the deep;
> When he made firm the skies above,
> when he fixed fast the springs of the deep;
> When he set for the sea its limit,
> so that the waters should not transgress his command;
> When he fixed the foundations of earth,
> then was I beside him as artisan;
> I was his delight day by day,
> playing before him all the while,
> Playing over the whole of his earth,
> having my delight with human beings.[88]

---

[88] Proverbs 8:22–31.

This passage is an ancient Hebrew account of Wisdom personified. How beautifully, though, we see in it Jesus, the Word of God made flesh to dwell with us, speaking with profound *love* and joy. He is the divine Artisan whose delight is with human beings. This is divine Wisdom, divine *Love*. This love, this joy, this *living heart of the universe* — Truth, Life, Way — this is Jesus Christ, the Lord.

How does all of this relate to a little strawberry?

Living within the Sacred Heart

In the lovely month of June, softly green and blossoming, when I bite into a freshly picked strawberry warm with the sun, I think of Jesus being there at its creation. This sweet red jewel of a fruit was loved into being through Christ for me to love it, too. In the shared union of our loving this berry, we meet each other — and we are one.

The same is true in my encounters with fellow human creatures. Each human person is powerfully loved into being through Christ and known intimately by Him, now and forever, as uniquely and particularly precious. When I, too, hold that person, like you, my dear reader, as precious, then, whether or not some judge you unlovable, whether or not you return my love, I am meeting Jesus in my loving of you.

Because He is loving you, too, utterly and completely.

When human love meets divine love, there is the Sacred Heart. There is the heart of reality, the point of the universe, the euphoric song of Heaven and Earth, the profound privilege and sacred wonder of being human, when God and I unite together in the loving of all things and all people: that is the living of eternal love that pierces through time and space.

It's Good to Be Here

In the Sacred Heart of Jesus, through this shared loving with God, we remember—and realize—something of the eternal truth of created life: that it is very, very good. The veil between Heaven and Earth slips partially from our eyes and we glimpse, for a moment, the terribly sacred beauty of where we are—where God in the flesh lived and loved—*lives and loves.* With our own hearts humbled by grace and filled with delight and gratitude, we sing out through the *whole* of our lives, in tremulous awe, "Lord, it's good to be here."

Acknowledgments

Every human being needs inspiration, encouragement, and assistance to discover who she is, what her God-given talents are, and how best to use them for her true fulfillment, which is the glory of God. And so, in this journey to become fully who God created me to be, my heart is filled with gratitude for many people, including every school teacher who recognized and nourished my mind inside my twisted body; every stranger who held open a door for me or called my gummy smile beautiful; every nurse's aide whose hands and heart helped me to heal and stay alive; and every priest who ever ministered the mysteries of God to me, whether or not I appreciated the power of the gift at the time.

I give my loving gratitude to my big sister, Carole Chase Lewis, for her love—for doting on me, helping to care for me, and being proud of me while keeping me humble; to Mary Parent O'Connell for her childhood and lifelong friendship that enabled me to feel the magic of being a real little girl; to Carl Lewis, for accepting and loving such an odd little stranger as his sister-in-law and for reading my blog; to my nephews, Matthew and Nathan, for giving me insight into the beautiful opening of their hearts and minds that reveal the shared wonders of human life, and for loving me; to my ancestors for being my ancestors;

to my extended family, especially my cousin, Jacqui Belleville, for being my fellow letter writer and confidant when I needed one; to my former aide and forever friend, Tammy Goodwin Berdal, for teaching me that there are some wounds that only God's love can heal; to Therese Williams, my newly discovered "twin," for her witness in reminding me to trust; to Donna De Guglielmo (DonnaMaria.org), for her friendship, inspiring life story, and encouraging influence; and to my mentor, the late John D. Meehan, for introducing me to my heart and profoundly changing my life in ways that he probably foresaw.

Many thanks to every follower of DivineIncarnate.com who encouraged me; to Maurice Billingsley for reaching through the blogging world to strengthen a little writer; to Sioux Lass for persistently asking for a book of my reflections; to Albert Salsich for blessing *It's Good To Be Here* as "a little manger" before it was even conceived; to Virginia Pillars, Laura Lowder, and Jeannie Ewing for giving their witness, advice, and support to share my own witness in a book; to Deacon Geoff Ashman for being the impetus of my first publicly shared work and, along with Matthew McSorley, Judith Gilbert, and Barbara Donovan, for test-reading and encouraging this book; and to Michelle Buckman for editing this book and leading this novice into a whole new world.

Always, I acknowledge, with grateful awe, that I am able to be who I am, love as I love, and write as I write because of the joyful love and amazingly devoted, willing sacrifices of my parents, Dan and Francine, who safeguard all that is good. And all that is good is created and gratuitously given by God, whom I, with all of my heart, soul, mind, and body, thank and praise for *everything*.

Sophia Institute

Sophia Institute is a nonprofit institution that seeks to nurture the spiritual, moral, and cultural life of souls and to spread the Gospel of Christ in conformity with the authentic teachings of the Roman Catholic Church.

Sophia Institute Press fulfills this mission by offering translations, reprints, and new publications that afford readers a rich source of the enduring wisdom of mankind.

Sophia Institute also operates the popular online resource CatholicExchange.com. *Catholic Exchange* provides world news from a Catholic perspective as well as daily devotionals and articles that will help readers to grow in holiness and live a life consistent with the teachings of the Church.

In 2013, Sophia Institute launched Sophia Institute for Teachers to renew and rebuild Catholic culture through service to Catholic education. With the goal of nurturing the spiritual, moral, and cultural life of souls, and an abiding respect for the role and work of teachers, we strive to provide materials and programs that are at once enlightening to the mind and ennobling to the heart; faithful and complete, as well as useful and practical.

Sophia Institute gratefully recognizes the Solidarity Association for preserving and encouraging the growth of our apostolate over the course of many years. Without their generous and timely support, this book would not be in your hands.

www.SophiaInstitute.com
www.CatholicExchange.com
www.SophiaInstituteforTeachers.org

Sophia Institute Press® is a registered trademark of Sophia Institute.
Sophia Institute is a tax-exempt institution as defined by the
Internal Revenue Code, Section 501(c)(3). Tax ID 22-2548708.